Learn Japanese Book for Beginners

Learn Practical & Conversational Japanese, Hiragana & Katakana

Contents

Arigatou!

Thank you for choosing to read this book, which contains the basics that you need to know and answers many practical and functional questions that you may encounter as you consider going to Japan, either for business or as part of a vacation. This book represents the totality of my experience in Japan and the information I believe I needed most while there. Your experience might differ, but what you learn in this book forms the basis of much of Japanese conversation. Knowing that, you'll be hard-pressed to find Japanese phrases more used than the ones contained herein. If you can get a grasp of the information presented in this book, you should be able to navigate most of the common situations you'll find yourself in.

If you make your way through this book and find that you really wish you had a bit more Japanese knowledge beyond even what you learn here, try out some of the resources and strategies presented in section 3. While you can get by in Japan based on what you'll learn in this guide, being even more prepared is never a bad thing. A full explanation of the Japanese writing system, including hiragana, katakana, and kanji, is presented at the end of this book to get you going in the right direction and also to serve as a reference if you need to read something written in Japanese.

SECTION 1: BASIC JAPANESE

INTRODUCTION

If you have picked up this book, it's likely that you are going to be visiting Japan, and perhaps you speak only minimal Japanese—if any at all. You will need a variety of phrases and gestures to be able to communicate effectively and smoothly, and for a beginner, this can present a significant challenge. It's easy for newcomers to the country to feel overwhelmed; from the complicated-looking kanji to the different intonation and pronunciation that Japanese offers, new speakers might think that there's no way they'll ever be able to communicate in Japanese. But the good news is that many interactions all share common traits, and by mastering just a few features of the Japanese language, you'll be able to get by in many situations.

This manual contains the most useful basic expressions that you will need in order to speak Japanese in Japan. It will enable you to be generally understood by those to whom you are speaking so that you can communicate the necessities. While you'll need to put in additional effort if you'd like to actually start having substantive conversations or making requests that involve more complex ideas, you should be able to survive in normal interaction after you've mastered the concepts presented in this book.

This manual represents the totality of my own experience in Japan as a tourist, student, employee, and individual after years of residence in the country. All of the Japanese contained herein is intended to be used in a variety of contexts, and so it has been simplified to be most useful while retaining a minimal, natural means of expression. It would be a great idea, if you're traveling to Japan for a specific purpose like business, to do a bit of research before you go and ensure you've got a "cheat sheet" of important words specific to you that you might need to know as well.

If you are looking for more substantive content to assist you with learning Japanese so that you can communicate even more clearly, see Section 3.

METHOD OF STUDY

When considering how much effort and time to dedicate to learning the material contained in this manual, understand that it varies for everyone. The best ways to familiarize yourself with the language are to listen and speak it whenever possible. For many people, two hours per week may be sufficient to master the information contained in this basic guide.

Memorization by repetition is at the heart of what is presented in this book, so at a minimum, it will be necessary to memorize the phrases and ideas in order to communicate the necessities while you're in Japan. If you dedicate yourself, one week should be enough to learn everything in this guide in preparation for your trip.

The good news is that the expressions found in this manual are general, everyday terminology, phrasing, and requests that exist independent of ideas of mood, so you won't ever have to worry about adapting what you're saying. Learn these phrases and you'll be set.

That being said, some people reading this guide are likely going to be heading off to Japan for a specific purpose. For some, that might be a business trip, and for others, it might be to tour the areas of Japan most associated with a certain facet of culture or history. In situations where you know you'll need specific language, it's best to come prepared by taking a look at some particular words unique to your own situation. If you're a businessman coming from an IT department, consider taking a little extra time to write down a small cheat sheet as a supplement to this guide with words you might want to know, like "computer," "network," and "administration."

HOW TO MASTER THE CONTENT OF THIS GUIDE

Japanese is by and large a difficult language, with a complex honorific system, a syllabary based upon 46 characters/sounds, and an alphabet made up of 2136 ideograms that bear significant meaning (those are called kanji). It is then easy to imagine that it may be difficult to understand and speak this language with fluency, smoothness, and understanding.

In order to communicate fluently in Japanese, you'll need to boost the volume of content that you can produce upon command. Good news, though—the volume of content that you'll need amounts to no more than 50 words. You could take five or six hours over a week to learn them and then be solidly on your way.

It's not necessary to memorize dozens of complex phrases, expressions, usages, and conjugations; use of your limited vocabulary will come through a combination of memorization, visualization, and practical content to ensure you master this material and are able to use it to complete a large variety of tasks in Japan.

STRUCTURE OF THE BOOK

This manual is divided into three sections.

- Section 1: Basic expressions
- Section 2: Situational Japanese
- Section 3: Additional help

The first section of the book focuses primarily on the actual building blocks that you will be learning in Japanese, absent of any context. You'll learn greetings and farewells, numbers, and basic words for items or ideas. This is the primary lesson in any course on Japanese.

The second section discusses a more practical approach to using the building blocks that you will have established in section 1. It shows the application of the words and phrases you learned so that you understand how they might appear in context.

The third section offers further resources to help fill in any gaps that you may have after you make your way through the book. If you need more Japanese for your specific situation, these aids will be a good place to start.

You may find that the first section is the most helpful to you.

PLANNING OUT YOUR WEEK(S) OF STUDY

It's important to go into any new project with a plan, and learning Japanese is no different. Decide the primary method that you will use to learn—whether that's rote memorization, flash cards, listening practice, or whatever works best for you—and figure out a time in your day when you can dedicate an hour or two exclusively to working with and understanding the content.

After even five hours in a week of practicing Japanese, you'll find that you have a much stronger grip on the language. Don't forget that you have a wide variety of options when it comes to practice; consider podcasts, YouTube, and online websites that will allow you to practice listening and reading.

THE PROPOSED STUDY PLAN

You can set up a plan that will work best for you, but here's a proposal to get you started:

- Two hours of watching native Japanese being spoken; this is very important, as it teaches you not only about cadence but also pronunciation and gets you accustomed to listening.
- 60 to 90 minutes of manual study. This includes memorization, recitation, and the typical work you associate with studying, like flash cards.
- 5 days where you can dedicate 15 to 20 minutes to a quick practical application. For example, perhaps during your lunch break, you can have a conversation with yourself where you pretend to order lunch in Japan.

Your plan might look something like this:

- **Monday**: Two hours of reading, watching videos, or listening to podcasts from 9:30 to 11:30
- **Tuesday**: 1 hour of studying vocabulary and phrases before dinner, from 4 to 5.
- **Thursday**: 1 hour of refining using your Japanese skills, such as following along with a video or using your vocabulary from 9 to 10, right before you go to bed.
- **Saturday and Sunday:** 15 minutes of actively using your Japanese that you've studied right when you get up, from 8 to 8:15.

1.1 WHICH PARTS OF JAPANESE ARE THE MOST IMPORTANT?

There are certain functional pieces of the Japanese language that you truly need to master – there's no avoiding them.

- Greetings
- Saying yes and no
- Saying thanks and apologizing
- Asking basic questions like "where" and "when"
- Numbers from 1 to 10

It's important that you develop a firm grasp on these concepts at a minimum, because they are going to be a significant part of what carries you through your interactions in Japanese. If you're looking for more specific, contextual situations where you might use yes and no, basic questions, and numbers, refer to the second part of the manual.

It's also critical that you do your best with the pronunciation of these elements. The good news is that they're relatively simply in pronunciation; just remember that these features are the backbone of your language. If people can't understand them, you'll have a hard time getting your meaning across.

Knowing this, Japanese people—especially if you'll be sticking to some of the more tourist-heavy areas like Tokyo and central Kyoto—are familiar with English pronunciation and may be able to guess what you're saying even if your pronunciation isn't quite right. Just do your best!

HOW MUCH JAPANESE DO YOU KNOW?

Take a minute to think about these questions.

- Do I have a friend who is studying Japanese with whom I could practice?

- Do I already know some Japanese, like how to say "hello" or "thank you"?
- How do you say "thank you" in Japanese?
- Can I count in Japanese already?

It's possible, depending on how exposed you've been to Japanese so far in your life, that you've already encountered words like konnichi wa, arigatou, and the numbers ichi, ni, and san.

GANBARIMASU!
I'LL DO MY BEST!

WHICH PHRASES DO I KNOW?

Take a look at the table below and see if you can pick out any phrases whose meanings you're already familiar with. You may take yourself by surprise at what you already know, but if nothing is familiar, that's all right too!

SUMIMASEN	**IRASSHAI MASE**
OHAYOU GOZAIMASU	**SAYOUNARA**
DOKO DESU KA?	**KONNICHI WA**
ONEGAI SHIMASU	**KONBAN WA**
ARIGATOU GOZAIMASHITA	**IKURA DESU KA?**
SUMIMASEN	**KONBINI ARIMASU KA?**

The assumption being made here is that you do, in fact, speak English; thus, these Japanese phrases have been broken up and formatted to facilitate an English speaker actually pronouncing them. Mastering Japanese pronunciation is one of the biggest parts of making yourself understood in Japan, so prepare your vocal cords to get practicing!

1.2 PRONUNCIATION AND GRAMMAR

The transcriptions used in this manual represent just one of many ways that Japanese as a language can be written down. The method used here is intended to optimize the readability and pronunciation of Japanese for new learners to encourage proper usage.

In essence, there are three ways to write down anything in Japanese: one with a native Japanese alphabet (kana), one using a direct transcription of those sounds (romaji), and one that is simply a phonetic version.

KANA: おはようございます！

ROMAJI: OHAYOU GOZAIMASU!

PHONETIC: OHAI-O GOZAI MAS

The romaji transcription method is the one chosen for this manual, and its rules will be explained and clarified as we go on. This helps to ensure consistency, as phonetic writing can suffer from a person's own biases about how something might be said. For example, in "ohai-o gozai mas," is "mas" pronounced like "moss" or like "mass"? For this reason, romaji will be used.

It's important to understand, too, that—thankfully!—Japanese letters always sound the same. In English, where "u" can sound like "uh" or "you" or "oo," it will always make the "oo" sound in Japanese. Without fail. Count on it. Talk about simplifying your learning! Let's take a look at the Japanese vowels and the sounds they make:

A: ah

E: eh

I: ee

O: oh

U: oo

Japanese contains some sounds that are not present in English; these include the silent u, the blended tsu, the long vowel, and the lengthened double consonant.

The silent u is likely the easiest to learn. When a word ends in *masu* or *desu*, the sound of the u is dropped (so that these words sound like "moss" and "dess"). However, pronouncing the u will still enable you to be understood; you may just sound slightly stilted.

The best way to describe blended tsu is via the word "tsunami," which is a word used in English that many people are already familiar with. It's common to pronounce this word as "soo na mi," but there's a little bit more nuance to it than that. Try saying the word "its." Now take the "ts" from that and use it in "tsunami." There's just a slight "t" right at the beginning that differentiates this piece of Japanese pronunciation.

In Japanese, long vowels are indicated by either two of the same vowels in a row (like *oneesan*) or the vowels "ou" together (like *kinou*). In both of these cases, you hold out the vowel sound for just a bit longer. It's not "kinoh," it's "kinoooooh."

Similarly, consonants can do the same thing. If two consonants appear together (like in *kitto*), you take a slight pause to make the consonant longer. This would result in the word *kitto* being pronounced "keet [pause] oh" instead of "keeto." Or the word *minna* being pronounced "meen [pause] a" instead of "meena."

As you continue to practice—and especially listen to—Japanese, the fine differences in these sounds will seem less daunting and more habitual. Don't give up!

At this point, you might already be feeling overwhelmed. That's understandable; there is a lot to take in when you're starting to learn a new language—especially Japanese, which is very different from English. You've probably heard people say that Japanese is a very hard language to learn, and maybe you're worried that it'll be tough to master the grammar.

If you're primarily focused on just getting by in Japan and hoping that some people will be able to speak English with you, skip ahead to section 1.3, where you'll be able to continue learning the basics of Japanese. If you'd like to take a little bit more of a deep dive into basic Japanese grammar—such as if you'd like to have some context for why things work the way they do—then stick around.

If you've heard Japanese so far in your life, you may have already picked up on some of the basics of grammar in the language. Six things in particular stand out as features that you may already be familiar with, and they're certainly ones that will inform all of the Japanese speaking and reading that you'll do as you travel to Japan.

THERE IS NO PLURAL

How can people go through life without being able to tell the difference between one and many? As it turns out, if you give it a try, you might find out that understanding how many of something you're talking about actually isn't as important as you might have thought. In Japanese, there is no use of the plural, at least on a regular basis. In other words, both "I saw a cute dog today" and "I saw a couple cute dogs today" would result in exactly the same sentence: *Kyou, kawaii inu wo mimashita* 今日、かわいい犬を見ました。

This lack of detail might really upset some people, and that's understandable. If it's really very important that you communicate that there are multiple of something, you can append *-tachi* to the end of a noun However, this is not a common tactic and is really only used for a couple of words on the regular; the majority of the time, number is assumed from context or just generally counted as unimportant. For example, *kodomo* 子供 (child) can become *kodomotachi* 子供たち (children).

VERBS COME AT THE END

If you've had any exposure to Japanese, you may have already noticed that unlike in English, the sentence order is inverted and words are placed in different locations. This is one of the most daunting features of

Japanese for newcomers, but give it a chance; you'll likely find it much simpler than you expect. Take, for example, "I went to the library." In English, this is represented by subject, verb, object: I > went > library. In Japanese, this sentence would be spoken or written as subject > object > verb: *watashi ha toshokan ni ikimashita* 私は図書館に行きました, or "I library went."

If you grow beyond this introductory guide to Japanese for tourists and branch out into more fluent Japanese, you may discover that inverting sentence order this way actually proves useful, as your important words (like verbs) never get lost in the hustle and bustle of the middle of a sentence.

YOU DON'T SAY "YOU"

Whether or not you're trying to expand your Japanese or simply get by in Japan, this point is very much worth consideration. It's true that Japanese uses a significantly reduced word count compared to English, and the word "you" is no exception. If you're talking to someone, it can often come across as rude or at least a bit impolite to just directly call them "you" (*anata,* あなた), even though English speakers would not find it out of place to say "What sort of movies do you like?" and similar. Most often, the best way to tackle this issue to either address a person by their title (like "doctor") or just completely leave out "you" altogether. That looks like this:

"Do you like cake?"

Anata *ha ke-ki ga suki desu ka?*	Avoid!
[Name]-san, ke-ki ga suki desu ka?	Perfect!
Ke-ki ga suki desu ka?	Fine!

You may wonder what to do if you don't know someone's name. The good news is that you don't need to! In the third example, the sentence just amounts to "like cake?" without the need for either a name or title. The reason this point is brought up in this book for tourists is because many "most important Japanese words" resources include *anata* as an example, because "you" is so common in English. However, these guides rarely explain how rarely *anata* is used and why.

THERE IS NO FUTURE TENSE

If you're worried about having to conjugate verbs as part of being understood in Japan, you can put that worry to rest. Japanese actually has no future tense all on its own. Instead, the future tense and the present tense are the same thing! That means that a Japanese listener will figure out your meaning from context, and you don't have to worry about any conjugation troubles with verbs. *Hon wo yomimasu* is both "I read a book" and "I will read a book." For that reason, saying that you will be going to a place when asking for directions just relies on you memorizing a phrase, not having to worry about how you work with your verbs.

IT'S EASY TO BE POLITE

If you're new to Japan, such as if you're traveling to the country for the first time, expecting to have to talk with people, or planning activities or meetings where you'll have to use some Japanese, you may be very worried that you'll come across as rude. After all, Japan is known as a very polite country, and it's common to hear that Japanese has a complex system of politeness built into its language. The good news is that there's no need for you to learn hyper-formal *keigo* or change the way you speak in order to humble yourself in your language; addressing basically everyone with verbs ending in *desu/masu* is more than sufficient to be polite. That's why all of the phrases and vocabulary used in this guide are put in this automatically polite form.

There is definitely a time for very formal and honorific language, but you're quite unlikely to encounter it during your trip to Japan, so take a deep breath and relax. Unless you're going to be speaking to the president of a large company, an important political figure, or someone with extremely high rank, you'll be able to use the phrases you've learned in this book with no problem. You're being polite already.

THERE ARE TWO KINDS OF ADJECTIVES

In English, an adjective is a word that is talking about a person, place, thing, or idea. It makes ideas broader by giving further detail, but in English, whether something is "blue," "giant," "spooky," or "rolling" doesn't matter. These words can all be talking about the word "ball."

In Japanese, however, adjectives are divided into two groups: *ii* adjectives and *na* adjectives. The only difference between them is that, as you might have been able to guess depending on how much you already know about Japanese, *ii* adjectives end with *ii* and *na* adjectives end with *na.*

The only reason this matters is for the sake of putting a sentence together; *na* adjectives drop the *na* sometimes (at the end of a sentence), but *ii* adjectives don't.

"That cat is pretty!" Pretty is *kirei na*, so this sentence would read *Sono neko ha kirei desu.* The *na* is allowed to be dropped.

"That dog is big!" Big is *ookii*, so this sentence would read *Sono inu ha ookii.* The *ii* has to stay.

The purpose of clarifying this is to give you some context; don't worry too much about memorizing these rules yourself. This guide is intended to give you the basics in an easily accessible and memorizable way. You won't need to enact these grammar rules on your own; they're merely here for background if it helps you.

By taking note of these simple grammar rules, you'll be able to have a better understanding of not only what you'll be learning moving forward in this guide but also *why* those things work. If those details aren't important to you, that's fine. For those who thrive in the *why* and *how*, this preemptive section should give you the background you need.

1.3 GREETINGS

Japanese is the language of "excuse me." There is a cultural centricity to the idea of being in someone's way, apologizing, or being humble in asking for help. For this reason, one of the most common (and most important) words to start with will be *sumimasen*. In about 90% of interactions, Japanese people will use *sumimasen* at least once.

SUMIMASEN

Excuse me, I'm sorry, thank you

If you're interrupting someone, asking a question, or generally just trying to get someone's attention, *sumimasen* is the word to lead with. If you don't know what to say, such as if you can't understand someone, it's *sumimasen*. This is by far the most useful word you'll have at your disposal; that's why Japanese people use it all the time as well. In fact, if you're not even sure what word to choose in any given situation, just try *sumimasen*. It's no exaggeration to say it'll probably be right.

Asking for directions: *sumimasen, eki wa doko desu ka?*

I'm sorry, where's the train station?

Accidentally bumping into someone: *sumimasen!*

Sorry about that!

Making a request: *sumimasen, mizu kudasai*

Sorry to bother, but could I have some water?

Trying to get someone's attention: *sumimasen!*

Excuse me!

HELLO! GOOD DAY! IN JAPANESE

In Japanese, the ideas of "hello" and "how are you" are often wrapped into a single thought. Or rather, it's unusual to explicitly ask a stranger how they're doing unless you already know them; Japan presents a "not my business" cultural attitude (you may have heard people refer to this as *kankei nai*) that respects people's privacy and doesn't interact in personal ways with strangers. In fact, you may hear Japanese people use this phrase in public. For example, if you pass by a couple who are arguing in a train station, people will generally not stop to see what's going on. They'll just mutter *kankei nai* ("it's not my business") and be on their way.

Because Japanese people are not typically interested in asking complete strangers how they're doing, if you find yourself needing to greet someone, you have three options:

OHAYOU GOZAIMASU	**GOOD MORNING**
KONNICHIWA	**GOOD AFTERNOON**
KONBANWA	**GOOD EVENING**

The *gozaimasu* in *ohayou gozaimasu* is a marker of formality; that's good, because you have no need to worry about moderating what level of politeness you're speaking at. This phrase will work on essentially everyone without fear of coming across as rude.

It's important to note that, like many other languages around the world (including English), some greetings can only be used at certain parts of the day. In English, this would be the difference between "good morning," "good afternoon," and "good evening." Japanese does the same thing, and with the same flexibility; no one is going to jump on you just because you used one half an hour past the standard "stopping" time for that phrase.

OHAYOU GOZAIMASU

From 5am to around 11am

KONNICHIWA

From noon to about 5pm

KONBANWA

From 6pm through the early morning hours

These three greetings will serve you at any time of day, so you'll be prepared to pull out the appropriate one based on what time of day it is. And don't worry—there is not a strict schedule in which these words can be used. Opting for *ohayou gozaimasu* instead of *konbanwa* at 3am isn't going to raise any eyebrows.

WHAT'S UP? HOW ARE YOU? IN JAPANESE

While you don't typically make "how are you" conversation on the train with strangers, you may occasionally find yourself wondering how to strike up a conversation with a new friend or check in on their day. For that, use *ogenki desu ka?*—a phrase that literally means "are you healthy?"

OGENKI DESU KA?

How are you?

Asking how someone is doing is generally reserved for family, friends, and close acquaintances. It's not the sort of thing that you say in passing to a cashier or restaurant server, for example. This differs somewhat significantly from how English works, as many English speakers are accustomed to small conversations with strangers—even small things like smiling quickly when you make eye contact with a stranger are not common in Japan.

Do you remember the four phrases you've learned so far?

OHAYOU GOZAIMASU

KONNICHIWA

KONBANWA

OGENKI DESU KA?

IRASSHAIMASE: WELCOME TO OUR LOCATION!

If you spend any length of time in Japan at all, you're likely to hear this phrase often—even within the first few minutes that you set foot in the country. It might be a relief, if you're feeling overwhelmed in your learning, to know that you yourself will never have to use this phrase; it's reserved only for a small subset of people. However, it's important to be able to recognize it so that you understand what's going on.

Whenever you walk into a grocery store, hotel, or other business, you'll likely be greeted with *irasshaimase!* This means "welcome to our store!" or similar. It's meant to get your attention and alert you to where the business' helpers are in case you need assistance and welcome you to the establishment. You are not expected to respond or say anything in return.

ARIGATOU GOZAIMASHITA

Thank you [for your visit]!

Just as you'll be greeted with *irasshaimase* when you enter an establishment, it's likely that you'll hear workers shout *arigatou gozaimashita* to thank you for visiting when you're leaving. Japan is a client-oriented or service-oriented society, so it's common to hear workers address you with thanks and appreciation for spending your time in their store. It's no wonder, then, that Japanese service-people commonly live by the phrase:

OKYAKU-SAMA WA KAMI-SAMA

Lit. "the customer is god"

SUMMARY OF GREETINGS

Here are a few of the most common greetings in Japan. Do you remember what they mean?

SUMIMASEN	KONNICHIWA	OHAYOU GOZAIMASU	KONBANWA

WHEN TO USE THESE EXPRESSIONS

Think about which of these expressions you might use in the following situations:

1. When you pass by the hotel reception at 9am on the way to the cafeteria

SUMIMASEN	KONNICHIWA	OHAYOU GOZAIMASU	KONBANWA

2. When you enter a café in the afternoon

SUMIMASEN	KONNICHIWA	OHAYOU GOZAIMASU	KONBANWA

3. When you stop by a restaurant to ask to see a menu

SUMIMASEN	KONNICHIWA	OHAYOU GOZAIMASU	KONBANWA

REMEMBER HOW TO USE PHRASES

In what situations would you use *sumimasen*? List as many as you can think of that you anticipate you might run into.

Which phrase are you most likely to hear when you enter a convenience store?

Listen to some Japanese commercials. Do you hear any of these phrases commonly?

1.4 SAYING GOODBYE

As explained in the previous section, because Japan is so service-oriented, the most common time that you will encounter farewell phrases is in the service sector—when you leave a store, after you check out at a hotel, or even when you disembark from a train. There is a cultural focus on "other" in Japan, and people are conditioned to understand that the client, customer, or visitor is a valued guest. Businesses are honored to have your attention. Some tourists get the impression that the enthusiasm and frequency with which they're thanked are fake or exaggerated, but this is simply not true. The culture of Japan is just built this way.

ARIGATOU GOZAIMASU

Thank you

The ending *gozaimasu* is what keeps this phrase formal and highly respectful, so expect to hear it used on you (the customer is god, remember?). When you check out at a hotel, it's likely the reception will thank you in this way. Similarly, if someone has done something kind for you, there's no shame in using this phrase right back at them!

SAYOUNARA

Goodbye

Saying goodbye using *sayounara* indicates that the speaker anticipates that you will be away for a long time; it doesn't convey the same tone as "see you later." Thus, you might hear airport workers wish you farewell saying *sayounara* when you board an airplane leaving Japan, but it's less likely you'll hear it from a convenience store cashier.

One cultural aspect that might take you by surprise is that workers often say all of these phrases in unison. It can be startling to leave a store and hear every worker simultaneously shout *arigatou gozaimashita* as you exit. This is just an intentional quirk; they're not trying to get your attention. It's common for all present workers to echo the same phrase, so don't be alarmed.

GOCHISOU SAMA IN RESTAURANTS

Arigatou gozaimasu and *sayounara* are two of the most common phrases you'll encounter during your time as a tourist in Japan. However, there's one special phrase used only in restaurants that it would be helpful to know.

GOCHISOU SAMA DESHITA

Thank you for the meal!

The *-sama* ending at the end of *gochisou* indicates formality, so you should have no worries about politeness when using this phrase. After you've eaten a meal, when you're done and don't plan to eat any more, saying *gochisou sama deshita* is a great way to not only say thanks but to indicate that the food was delicious, your compliments to the chef.

EXERCISES WITH PHRASES

Do you remember these important expressions? Try to practice what they mean:

SUMIMASEN

ARIGATOU GOZAIMASU

SAYOUNARA

GOCHISOU SAMA DESHITA

Try explaining to a friend or family member what sort of jobs or tasks they might be doing in Japan when they hear or have to use these phrases:

SUMIMASEN

ARIGATOU GOZAIMASU

SAYOUNARA

GOCHISOU SAMA DESHITA

1.5 SAYING YES AND NO

Japan as a culture is dictated in large part by the desire not to disturb the status quo or cause a disturbance in general. It's not considered normal to depart too heavily from social norms, and thus, it's much more common to agree than to disagree.

If one wishes to express disagreement or say no to a request or suggestion, this can certainly be achieved, although in a more roundabout way. An extended silence may often be interpreted as "no," but otherwise, simply reasoning your way out of a situation is also common. In other words, leaving your answer at "no" is not as typical as saying something like, "No, I'm quite all right, thanks."

THE SCALE OF EXPRESSIONS

Take a look at some of these phrases to use when you want to say yes or no.

HAI	Yes
HAI, SOU DESU	Yes, that's right
CHIGAIMASU	That's not quite right
DAIJOUBU DESU	It's okay/I'm fine

As you can see, there are many ways to say "no" or convey your meaning without being direct. Unlike in English, where turning something into the negative is as simple as adding the word "no" or "not," there is no equivalent in Japanese. You cannot simply add a single word to a sentence to make it negative, as in English.

WHEN TO USE *HAI*

Hai, or the direct "yes," is a strong term that can be used to mean unequivocal agreement or assent. It is a statement of fact and less of opinion; keep this in mind when saying "yes" in Japan.

Similarly, *hai, sou desu* literally means, "Yes, that's right" or "Yes, you've gotten that correct." This is more commonly used when someone is confirming information with you—for example, if you're ordering at a restaurant and a server repeats your order.

WHEN TO USE *CHIGAIMASU*

The word *chigaimasu* literally means "it's different," but in the context of a conversation, it's commonly used to express that something didn't go as expected or was misunderstood. For example, if you're at a train station buying a ticket for Kyoto station and the station attendant confirms, "So you want to go to Nara station," you're free to butt in with *chigaimasu* to indicate, "Actually, that's not right."

WHEN TO USE *DAIJOUBU DESU*

The word *daijoubu* has many meanings, including "all right" and "don't worry about it." For this reason, it can be a complicated structure to use. It is most commonly pulled out in conversation to signal that you'd rather not participate in something that's happening—it's a common way to say, "I'm all right, I'm good, I'll sit this one out." If someone offers you food and you're not hungry, *daijoubu desu*.

SITUATION: IN THE CAFÉ

Imagine that you're in a café. You've been wandering around Japan in the fall, and it's a bit chilly, so you're hoping to pick up some warm coffee and relax for a bit. You may be able to use some of the phrases you've just learned to get you through a conversation after you've ordered your hot coffee.

AISU KOOHII DESU!

Here's your iced coffee!

CHIGAIMASU... HOTTO KOOHII DESU.
SUMIMASEN

Oh, that's not quite right... I ordered a hot coffee.
Sorry about that!

Pointing out an error using *chigaimasu* is helpful, but it also creates a situation in which the listener has to acknowledge that they've done something wrong. For this reason, it's common to use *sumimasen* at the same time in order to convey that you're not angry about the mistake and that you're sorry for causing the inconvenience to fix it.

SITUATION: BEING OFFERED ALCOHOL

Imagine that you're out with some friends in Japan, and they've just grabbed some alcohol from a store and would like to share. If you don't drink, are too young to drink, or simply don't want some, you could find yourself in a pickle. Check out how to navigate through this conversation.

OSAKE WA IKAGA DESU KA?

Would you like to have some alcohol?

DAIJOUBU DESU

I'm okay, thanks

While *daijoubu desu* can be used to indicate that you're doing well or that everything's okay, in this context, it takes on the related meaning of "no thank you." That being said, let's check out another way to use *daijoubu*.

SITUATION: LOOKING FOR POTATOES

Imagine it: you go to Japan, and you're in a fast food restaurant. You're hoping to get some French fries, but you don't see any in the pictures on the menu.

SUMIMASEN,
FURAI POTATO, ARIMASU KA?

Excuse me, do you have French fries?

AH, SUMIMASEN! ARIMASEN

Ah, I'm sorry! We don't

DAIJOUBU DESU

Oh, that's okay!

As you can see, context plays a big part in determining what meaning *daijoubu desu* will take on.

SEEING JAPANESE VIA EXPRESSIONS

The vocabulary and phrasing of any language is important, but especially in Japan, body language and physical expression are equally important in conveying meaning. As you have seen, some phrases have more than one meaning, and how you posture yourself when delivering them can help to ensure that your intended meaning is understood.

1.6 TO THANK AND APOLOGIZE

Japanese contains multiple phrases to express apology and thanks, but the two most common are:

SUMIMASEN

ARIGATOU GOZAIMASU

ABOUT THANKS AND APOLOGIES

Because Japan is a "consideration" culture in which a lot of focus and attention is paid to how you're making other people feel, words of thanks and apology are extremely common and frequently used. It's nearly ubiquitous, for example, to hear not only *sumimasen* but also *arigatou* and *irasshaimase* (remember that one?) around town and in TV commercials.

SUMIMASEN
I'm sorry

ARIGATOU GOZAIMASU
Thank you

As odd as it may seem, *sumimasen* can also function as a way to say *arigatou*. How can you use apology to convey thanks? Imagine a situation in which you cause trouble for someone—such as when you point out they've gotten your order wrong and they have to remake it. In this situation, when they return with the correct order, it would be fine to say *sumimasen*, or in other words, "Sorry about that, I appreciate you going out of your way!"

SITUATIONS

When someone picks up your umbrella and brings it to you so you don't leave it behind:

SUMIMASEN, ARIGATOU GOZAIMASU!

Oh sorry, thanks so much!

When someone helps you check out at a hotel:

SUMIMASEN! ARIGATOU GOZAIMASU. SAYOUNARA!

Sorry to be such trouble! Thanks for your help. Goodbye!

When someone assists you with a task, like buying you a train ticket while you're filling out the paperwork for your Japan Rail Pass so you can make your train on time:

SUMIMASEN, TASUKARIMASU!

Sorry, you're a lifesaver!

Tasukarimasu literally means "you save me," and it's used when someone is doing you a favor that really helps you out.

When a friend invites you out for dinner and pays for your portion:

ARIGATOU GOZAIMASU!
GOCHISOU SAMA DESHITA!

You've already had one run-in with *gochisou sama deshita*, and it's a great way to convey your thanks while eating.

Arigatou gozaimasu and *sumimasen* are two slightly different forms of thanks. *Sumimasen* is also a very formal way to apologize, so you'll see it used in a variety of situations.

Think back and try to practice these two very important phrases:

SUMIMASEN
ARIGATOU GOZAIMASU

APOLOGIES REGARDING INTENTION

Arigatou and *sumimasen* are two ways to let someone know you appreciate them tolerating a situation, but there's another phrase that is equally crucial in conveying apology, and it has to do with your unintentional mistakes.

GOMEN NASAI

I'm sorry

Gomen nasai is used most commonly when you've troubled someone and honestly didn't mean to, or if it was intentional, they went very far out of their way to accommodate.

GOMEN NASAI

I'm sorry

Think about a situation where you step on someone's dress and accidentally rip it or elbow someone in the ribs while getting on a train. These are unintentional situations where you've really put someone out, and they're a great opportunity for *gomen nasai*.

GOMEN NASAI VS. SUMIMASEN

It's clear that these two phrases can be used in very similar circumstances, so how can you tell the difference in which one to choose? In general, you can think of it like this: *sumimasen* most commonly appears when you ask for something intentionally, and *gomen nasai* is for those unintentional accidents.

SUMIMASEN

GOMEN NASAI

You can also think of it another way: *sumimasen* is a soft form meaning "sorry for the inconvenience" or "I appreciate it," while *gomen nasai* is a true "I'm sorry."

EXERCISES

Which form of apology is appropriate in the following situations?

When you bump into someone on the train:

SUMIMASEN OR GOMEN NASAI

When someone brings you the wrong order at a restaurant:

SUMIMASEN OR GOMEN NASAI

When you're trying to get the attention of the staff at a hotel:

SUMIMASEN OR GOMEN NASAI

When you knock someone's phone out of their hand and it lands on the hard street:

SUMIMASEN OR GOMEN NASAI

1.7 BASIC QUESTIONS

Every language has basic ways of discovering information that are used in dozens of situations throughout the day. In English, these are the who/what/when/where/why words, and Japanese in many ways mirrors this convention. However, unlike English, Japanese question words may change slightly depending on context. The good news is that by memorizing the question in its entirety, you'll never have to worry about how to change up the question words yourself!

NAN DESU KA?

What is that?

DOKO DESU KA?

Where [is that]?

IKURA DESU KA?

How much does that cost?

[KOOHII] DESU KA?

Is that [coffee]?

DAIJOUBU DESU KA?

Is that okay?

All questions in formal or polite Japanese will end in either *desu ka* or word+*masu ka*. "Ka" is a particle that you can add on to the end of any sentence to make it a question. Think of it like a verbal question mark. You don't need to change anything else about the sentence—just add *ka* and it becomes a question.

WHERE/WHAT/HOW MUCH

Nan, doko, and *ikura* are probably the three most common question words you'll use if you spend any time in Japan as a tourist.

NAN DESU KA?

What is that?

DOKO DESU KA?

Where [is that]?

IKURA DESU KA?

How much does that cost?

Can you tell that "desu ka" is roughly equivalent to the "is this?" part of the phrases? *Desu* is Japanese's "being verb" just like "is" works in English. Am, is, are, was, were, be, being, and been are all the forms of "is" in English, and what's great about Japanese is that *desu* serves the role of essentially all of those all on its own!

IS THIS COFFEE?

Two of the most important phrases that will serve you during your time in Japan are:

DESU KA* AND *ARIMASU KA

But what's the difference?

Desu ka is used when speaking of things that "are." It is a being verb: am/is/are. It's a very basic question.

KOOHII DESU KA?

Is that coffee?

WASABI DESU KA?

Is that wasabi?

BAKA DESU KA?

Are you dumb?

KARAI DESU KA?

Is this spicy?

DO YOU HAVE THAT?

Arimasu ka signifies "have." It's a word of possession or "existence," and it works to indicate if someone has something or if something exists (like if "there is" wifi at a certain location). It's the question you can ask servicepeople to confirm their services.

WIFI ARIMASU KA?

Do you have wifi?

KAFE LATE ARIMASU KA?

Do you have café lattes?

BEJITARIAN NO MENU ARIMASU KA?

Do you have a vegetarian menu?

IS THAT OKAY?

The ultimate question for confirmation of permission is asking, "Is that okay?" In Japanese, there is one primary way to ask this:

DAIJOUBU DESU KA?

Is that okay? Is it all right?

You can swap "daijoubu" with "okay" (yes, the English word) and still be understood, but *daijoubu* is much more contextually natural. "Okay" (often spelled in Japanese as *OK* or *okkee*) is pronounced the same as in English because it is a borrowed word.

THE INTERESTING ORIGIN OF DAIJOUBU

The origin of the word *daijoubu* is actually fascinating, and it might not mean what you think. The kanji used to make up the word mean 大 large 丈 strong 夫 husband and originally come from China. (Most kanji come from China, as Japan borrowed a significant part of its early written language from the country.)

大丈夫

DAIJOUBU

BIG STRONG HUSBAND

In antiquity, having a very large, very strong man of the house ensured protection and a solution to some problems in the home.

In these times, one answer to the question, "Is everything going well with you?" was "I have a big husband!" In other words, "Yep, I'm okay, I'm safe and protected."

This is why the phase has morphed over time to mean "okay" or "all right," and it's why it can also be posed as a question. "Do you have a big strong husband?"

DAIJOUBU DESU KA?

Is everything all right?

1.8 NUMBERS IN JAPANESE

The numbers from one (*ichi*) to ten (*jyuu*) are all you need to count all the way to 99. If you understand the basics, you'll be counting up a storm in no time, because Japanese numbers build on each other. You can put them together by combining the pieces into something bigger.

ICHI – NI – SAN

1 – 2 – 3

YON – GO – ROKU

4 – 5 – 6

NANA – HACHI

7 – 8

KYUU – JYUU

9 – 10

To say "one," use *ichi*. If you want to say "eleven," just put the pieces together: 10 + 1, or *jyuu* + *ichi*. Thus, eleven is *jyuuichi*. Can you guess what 48 would be? *Yonjyuu hachi*, or "four tens [40] and an eight."

NUMBERS FROM 20 TO 100

20	NI JYUU
30	SAN JYUU
40	YON JYUU
50	GO JYUU
60	ROKU JYUU
70	NANA JYUU
80	HACHI JYUU
90	KYUU JYUU
100	HYAKU

The same principles work once you go above a hundred; four hundred would literally be “four + hundred,” or *yon hyaku*.

1.9 HOW TO READ PRICES

One of the most typical uses you'll have for understanding numbers as a visitor to Japan is when interpreting prices. In general, prices are going to follow the same rules as normal numbers; however, there are just a few exceptions.

The word for "one thousand" is *sen*, and one hundred is *hyaku*. Understanding that, check out the table below and see how the words fit together as building blocks in the same way normal counting works.

1110	**SEN**	**HYAKU**	**JYUU**
1220	**SEN**	**NI HYAKU**	**NI JYUU**
1330	**SEN**	**SAN BYAKU**	**SAN JYUU**
1440	**SEN**	**YON HYAKU**	**YON JYUU**
1550	**SEN**	**GO HYAKU**	**GO JYUU**
1660	**SEN**	**ROPPYAKU**	**ROKU JYUU**
1770	**SEN**	**NANA HYAKU**	**NANA JYUU**
1880	**SEN**	**HAPPYAKU**	**HACHI JYUU**
1990	**SEN**	**KYUU HYAKU**	**KYUU JYUU**

As you can see, some of these terms have a special conjugation only in the presence of certain numbers. Check them out in more detail:

NUMBERS FROM 200 TO 1000

200	NI HYAKU
300	**SAN BYAKU**
400	YON HYAKU
500	GO HYAKU
600	**ROPPYAKU**
700	NANA HYAKU
800	**HAPPYAKU**
900	KYUU HYAKU
1000	SEN

Be careful of the three exceptions to the rule:

300: SAN BYAKU

600: ROPPYAKU

800: HAPPYAKU

EXERCISE: READING PRICES

Take a look at these Japanese prices. They're going to be some common amounts you might spend on typical items at cafés, convenience stores, and train stations. Remember: in Japan, credit cards are rarely accepted, so you'll have to count out your cash.

450 円	**570 円**	**680 円**
690 円	**710 円**	**740 円**
840 円	**940 円**	**1220 円**
1560 円	**1720 円**	**1880 円**

The kanji 円 is "yen," pronounced *en* in Japanese. Just like in English, you can add the word "en" to the end of any amount just like you would "dollars."

PREVIOUS EXERCISE: ANSWERS

450 EN: YON HYAKU GO JYUU EN

570 EN: GO HYAKU NANA JYUU EN

680 EN: ROPPYAKU HACHI JYUU EN

690 EN: ROPPYAKU KYUU JYUU EN

710 EN: NANA HYAKU JYUU EN

740 EN: NANA HYAKU YON JYUU EN

840 EN: HAPPYAKU YON JYUU EN

940 EN: KYUU HYAKU YON JYUU EN

1220 EN: SEN NI HYAKU NI JYUU EN

1560 EN: SEN GO HYAKU ROKU JYUU EN

1720 EN: SEN NANA HYAKU NI JYUU EN

1880 EN: SEN HAPPYAKU HACHI JYUU EN

Take a look back and see how you did! You'll do best if you practice until you can recite a price in just a few seconds. One great way to help practice is to start writing down important numbers on Post-It notes. For example, if you have to call the pharmacy later, find their number and write it down using the Japanese spelling of the numbers. Later, when you go to call, you'll have to practice translating it back in order to place the call.

NUMBERS AND COUNTERS

The idea of counters is likely foreign to most native English speakers, as English doesn't really use the concept. In Japanese, numbers can't always be used alone when counting objects or items. A long, tall object has a different "counter," or marker that goes with the number, than a person does. Thankfully, for the majority of your needs in Japan as a tourist, you won't have to worry about learning individual counters like *mai, hon*, and *pun* (for flat objects, long objects, and minutes, respectively).

Instead, focus your efforts on learning multi-purpose counting words.

BIIRU, HITOTSU KUDASAI

One beer, please!

In Japanese, if you're just generally trying to say how many of a thing you want—which is going to be one of the most common reasons you'll use numbers when speaking—you get to choose from a special set of words.

HITOTSU = 1 **FUTATSU = 2**
MITSU = 3 **YOTSU = 4**
ITSUTSU = 5

You can't simply say "one beer, please" by saying *biiru ichi kudasai*! You'll probably be understood (maybe), but you won't be correct. Instead, check out the difference between when to use numbers and when to use counters:

HOTTO KOOHII, HITOTSU KUDASAI!

One hot coffee, please!

KOOHII, HYAKU EN DESU.

That coffee is 100 yen.

BIIRU, HITOTSU KUDASAI!

One beer, please!

HOTTO KOOHII, FUTATSU KUDASAI!

Two hot coffees, please!

DOONATSU, MITSU KUDASAI!

Three donuts, please!

ASKING FOR THE BILL

Now that you've learned numbers, you're on your way to easily understanding a restaurant or grocery store bill. If you're at a bar or restaurant, you can call for your bill (in fact, it's likely you'll need to call or just go to the front counter pay, as they don't often bring bills to the table as they do in many English-speaking countries due to the much rarer use of credit cards).

SUMIMASEN

Excuse me

KAIKEI ONEGAI SHIMASU

Could I have the bill, please?

It's not usually particularly important that you listen closely to the amount told to you, as you'll also be shown the amount owed via a paper bill or electronic system.

SUMIMASEN, IKURA DESU KA?

Excuse me, how much does this cost?

If you're still having trouble understanding what your bill comes to, it never hurts to ask for clarification about how much something costs.

MORE PRACTICE

KOOHII WA HYAKU EN DESU.

It's 100 yen for coffee.

KOOHII WA HYAKU EN NI NARIMASU.

That coffee will come to 100 yen.

This second option is a more formal variant that you may encounter; don't let it throw you off!

Remember that some numbers behave differently depending on their context; take some time to practice the following table to make sure you've gotten your pronunciation down.

100 円 HYAKU EN

150 円 HYAKU GO JYUU EN

180 円 HYAKU HACHI JYUU EN

1200 円 SEN NI HYAKU EN

1500 円 SEN GO HYAKU EN

1800 円 SEN **HAPPYAKU** EN

2500 円 NI SEN GO HYAKU EN

SECTION 2: SITUATIONAL JAPANESE

2.1 WHEN AND WHY TO SPEAK JAPANESE

The objective for learning to speak Japanese is probably clear: to be a helpful and easy to interact with tourist in Japan, and to understand Japanese as it's being spoken to you. This will offer you more opportunities for fun activities and experiences while in the country and make you generally easier to be around.

Unlike some of the very direct speech common in English, understand that Japanese has a roundabout way of accomplishing things in conversation. For that reason, it's important that you are conscious not only of the way you use Japanese but also the way others around you are using it toward you. Being direct, raising your voice when something doesn't go your way, and similar actions are going to be highly frowned upon. Remember that Japan as a culture is other-focused, not self-focused. You are always imposing when you ask for help. The waitress is always imposing upon you when she repeats your order back to you to confirm. It's a culture of humility of self.

JAPANESE AND ENGLISH

There are differences in the way Japanese and English people typically study each other's respective languages that influence how each will talk to the other. In English-speaking countries, most speakers learn Japanese with the goal of communicating in the country or being able to interact with its cultural materials (think being able to read manga, watch anime, listen to J-pop, and so on). Sure, they may take tests and study the language through formal education, but they come into Japanese typically as an elective class that they're taking out of interest. Japanese as a foreign language is rarely forced upon English speakers as a class that they have to take.

In Japan, in contrast, English is a subject where the primary goal is just to get a good grade. English is part of the national curriculum, and all Japanese students are required to take at least a little English. Naturally, some Japanese people are going to be extremely interested in English, just as English-speaking people are interested in Japanese. However, it's important to understand that because English is just a class for most Japanese people, their ability to handle idioms, turns of phrase, and other casual or complex ways of speaking in English might not be the same as your ability to dish them out.

A POWERFUL JAPANESE PHRASE

NIHONGO, DAIJOUBU DESU

I'm okay at Japanese

If you encounter someone in Japan who begins speaking to you in English (which many people might try to do, in order to be helpful) but you find that they're having trouble communicating or being understood, there's nothing you can say to them more comforting than *nihongo, daijoubu desu*. This lets them know that it's all right to try having the conversation with you in Japanese instead.

It may still be a struggle for you to understand them, but if you work together in both English and Japanese, you may just get your point across. If you want to say that it's no problem using Japanese, *nihongo, daijoubu desu* is the way to do it.

This may be especially true for you if you plan to make stops in large cities like Tokyo, Osaka, and Kobe. Public-facing Japanese workers like taxi drivers will often attempt to strike up conversations in English, but because they haven't always had a full English conversation, it may end up being *more* confusing for you despite their best, well-intentioned (and likely much appreciated!) efforts. In this case, saying that you may also be able to speak a bit in Japanese can help them to be at ease.

MOST FRUSTRATING SITUATIONS FOR TOURISTS

A couple situations stand out to many tourists as the most frustrating encounters they have while in the country, and for most people, these experiences are the same. The most frequent ones are:

- When they are forced to rely on a local speaking to them in English or speaking for them in Japanese to others because they can't make themselves be understood
- When they have to use a mix of English and gestures or hand motions to get their point across because their Japanese is failing them
- When they have to look up everything in an online dictionary before they can communicate

Many of these situations can be avoided with just a bit of practice. It'll be unavoidable to encounter a few areas that are unfamiliar once you get to Japan, but if you can have the confidence to say *nihongo, daijoubu desu* and really mean it, you'll be well ahead of the curve.

2.2 QUESTIONS FOR THE STREET

Because you'll be in a new place, you may find yourself disoriented or even lost while trying to get to where you're going in Japan. These phrases will help to get you out of that pickle.

MOVEMENT EXPRESSIONS

SUMIMASEN	Excuse me
KOKO DESU KA?	Is it here?
CHIKAI DESU KA?	Is it nearby?
TOOI DESU KA?	Is it far?
DOKO DESU KA?	Where is it?
ARIMASU KA?	Do you have it?
IKIMASU KA?	Shall we go? *or* Does this go to?

Give yourself some time to practice. As you review your itinerary for your trip, try out these phrases by asking yourself in Japanese if you've arrived at your destination, how far it is, and so on.

SITUATION: WHERE IS AKIHABARA?

Let's have a look at an example situation in which you've arrived in Japan and you're looking to check out the sights and stores in Akihabara—which you may very well be planning to do in reality! It's a very popular, bustling location.

If you're traveling to Japan for any of the most common reasons, like enjoying the culture, you'll likely want to make a stop at Akihabara. Radio Kaikan is a huge building full of stores, and the entire area is alive with bustling shopping options. It's the central location for all of Japan's most popular foreign markets, like trading cards, anime, and manga, and it's also a very famous area for electronics. It wouldn't be a surprise at all that you'd be interested in making a stop there, since it's easily accessed from Tokyo's circular Yamanote train line.

So let's say you've been eagerly awaiting your trip to Akihabara. You've gotten yourself a bit lost after not catching the name of the train station you got off at on accident, so you're wondering if you've actually made it to Akihabara. Don't forget to lead into the conversation politely to get people's attention.

SUMIMASEN

Excuse me

KOKO, AKIHABARA DESU KA?

Am I in Akihabara? [lit. "Is this Akihabara?"]

AKIHABARA, DOKO DESU KA?

Where is Akihabara?

AKIHABARA, CHIKAI DESU KA?

Is Akihabara nearby?

Those questions are all you'll need in order to figure out where to go, as any answers can either be given in enough English for you to understand (especially if you ask a train station attendant) or with gestures that are universal, like pointing to where you need to go next.

SITUATION: WHERE'S THE CAFÉ?

Imagine this: you're tired after a long flight to Japan, and you're trying to buy tickets to an event tomorrow, but it's already so late at night that a lot of businesses are closed. If you just had some Wifi, you'd be set! So you head out to look for a 24-hour café that might have Wifi.

SUMIMASEN

Excuse me

CHIKAKU NI KAFE, ARIMASU KA?

Is there a café nearby?

CHIKAKU NI COMBINI, ARIMASU KA?

Is there a convenience store nearby?

STARBUCKS, DOKO DESU KA?

Where is there a Starbucks?

The phrase *doko desu ka* is useful in establishing not only the presence of something you're looking for but also the first steps in finding it.

SITUATION: DOES THIS ROAD GO TO THE TEMPLE?

In this context, pretend that you're on your way to see a very famous Japanese temple in Kiyomizu—it's highly recommended. You're on your phone looking at a map, but you're running low on battery, and you won't be able to use the phone for the entire time.

SUMIMASEN

Excuse me

KORE, KIYOMIZUDERA NI IKIMASU KA?

Does this lead to Kiyomizu temple?

KIYOMIZUDERA, CHIKAI DESU KA?

Is Kiyomizu temple nearby?

KIYOMIZUDERA, TOOI DESU KA?

Is Kiyomizu temple far from here?

ARIGATOU GOZAIMASU

Thanks so much

The word *kore* indicates "this," or something that is nearby in relation to your position. In this context, it's helpful because it indicates which path or road you're talking about.

KORE

This

Kore is also very helpful in the public transport sector, where "this" comes in handy to ask about buses, trains, and other transport.

KORE, KIYOMIZUDERA NI IKIMASU KA?

Does this [train, bus, etc.] go to Kiyomizu temple?

SITUATION: EXPRESSING THANKS

Earlier, you learned about *arigatou gozaimasu* as the way of saying "thank you very much" when people answer your questions, come to your aid, or offer help. While it's completely fine to leave your thanks at *arigatou gozaimasu*, if you're feeling particularly helped by someone, you can add on to the phrase to increase the emotiveness and indicate how truly thankful you are for the help.

SUMIMASEN

Excuse me

ARIGATOU GOZAIMASU, TASUKARIMASHITA!

Thanks so much, you really saved me!

HONTOU NI ARIGATOU GOZAIMASU!

Really and truly, thank you so much!

Tasukarimashita means "rescued" or "saved," and *hontou ni* is a way of adding seriousness to a phrase. It means something close to "truly."

JAPANESE-MODIFIED ENGLISH

The Japanese language is not restricted to only native Japanese words. In fact, Japanese has an entire alphabet separate from its native characters dedicated to writing down foreign loan words. For this reason, it's not uncommon to find an English word or two as you go about your day in Japan.

OK DESU KA?

Ok?

DON MAI!

Don't worry about it!

CHIKETTO

Ticket

OK desu ka carries the same meaning as *daijoubu desu ka*, and *don mai* comes from the English "don't mind." See if you can spot other English words as you listen to Japanese.

FOTO, DAIJOUBU DESU KA?

Is it okay to take a photo?

FOTO, OK DESU KA?

Is it okay to take a photo?

PRACTICE AND VISUALIZATION

As always, it's helpful to take some time and imagine yourself in the situations where you might need to rely on these phrases. There's no need for you to get things exactly perfect, but the closer you can get to an authentic Japanese phrase, the easier you'll be to understand. Plus, people will appreciate the extra effort.

EXERCISES

- Situation: Where is Yodobashi Camera?
- Situation: Where is the bar?
- Situation: Does this road go to the club?
- Situation: Thanking someone who found your wallet
- Situation: When your Japanese is fine and you don't have to worry

Visualizing your responses to these situations will help you to stay calm and successfully memorize the information before you head to Japan! It will also help you feel less like a fish out of water when the time finally comes to say the things you've been practicing.

2.3 CHECKING INTO A HOTEL

Hotels are on the forefront of civilized travel, and they're a huge part of what makes an experience as a tourist relaxing, memorable, and fun. A great hotel is going to have a big impact on a good trip. We all know how hotels work, from the helpful front desk staff to checking in, holding luggage, and cleaning rooms. In Japan, hotel staff are more likely to speak English than passersby on the street, but your experience during your stay will be even easier if you're familiar with some key Japanese phrases.

EXPRESSIONS

SUMIMASEN	Excuse me
ONEIGAI SHIMASU	Please
ARIMASU KA?	Do you have / is there?
YOYAKU SHITEIMASU	I have a reservation
NIMOTSU ONEGAI SHITAI DESU, DAIJOUBU DESU KA?	Would it be all right to leave my luggage here?

These phrases will be the most helpful during your stay in a hotel.

SEQUENCE OF EVENTS: ENTERING A HOTEL

In general, entering a hotel goes the same way every time.

KONNICHIWA
Hello

SUMIMASEN
Excuse me

ONEGAI SHIMASU
Please

You'll see this, for example, if you just get off a train and walk to your hotel. You'll enter and be greeted with *Konnichiwa*, which you can say in return. Then, you might walk up to the desk and apologize with *sumimasen* as you search for your hotel reservation confirmation. Then, you'll be able to use *onegai shimasu* to say that you'd love to leave your luggage until your check-in time.

USEFUL EXPRESSIONS IN HOTELS

Hotel workers are there to be helpful, and you may find that you'll need their assistance during your stay.

[SERVICE] ARIMASU KA?

Do you offer [service]?

[SERVICE] ONEGAI SHIMASU

Could I please have [service]?

[SERVICE] DOKO DESU KA?

Where can I find [service]?

It may be helpful for you not only to practice these phrases but also to jot them down. It will be easy to take a peek at your notes while you're rifling through the paperwork confirming your check-in! Also have in mind any particular locations you hope to visit or services that you're sure you need so that you can figure out how to express that idea before you even get there.

SITUATION: CHECKING IN AND OUT OF A HOTEL

The Japanese language borrows English for the terms "check in" (*chekku in*) and "check out" (*chekku auto*, pronounced "out-o"). You can use this phrase as part of your complete check-in dialogue.

KONNICHIWA

Hello

SUMIMASEN

Excuse me

CHEKKU IN ONEGAI SHIMASU

I'd like to check in, please

JACOB DE YOYAKU SHITEIMASU

I have a reservation for Jacob

Yoyaku means "reservation," and *shiteimasu* means "I've made" or "I've done" in this context. So you would literally be saying "I've made a reservation for Jacob."

SITUATION: ACQUIRING SERVICES AT THE HOTEL

Sometimes, at a hotel, you'll need help with more than just checking in or finding a place to store your luggage. In these cases, remember that especially in Japan, hotel workers are ready to assist and happy to help with anything you need.

SUMIMASEN

Excuse me

RUUM KII ONEGAI SHIMASU

Could I please have a room key?

HEYA BANGOO ONEGAI SHIMASU

Could you please tell me my room number?

CHEKKU AUTO ONEGAI SHIMASU

I'd like to check out, please

WAIFAI ARIMASU KA?

Do you have wifi?

PASWAADO ARIMASU KA?

Is there a password [in other words, "could I have the internet password, please?"]

ATM ARIMASU KA?

Is there an ATM?

ARIGATOU GOZAIMASU

Thank you

You'll see that in many of these phrases, the most important part is *arimasu ka*.

ARIMASU KA?

Do you have?

2.4 WHEN RIDING IN A TAXI

The good news about traveling in Japan nowadays is that thanks to the advent of GPS technology, it's no longer required that tourists understand how to say complex phrases like "take a left at the second intersection and then continue for two kilometers." What's important when giving and receiving directions is simply the ability to convey ideas like "over there," "here," and, for the sake of taking a taxi, "how much does this cost?"

EXPRESSIONS

-MADE ONEGAI SHIMASU	To [destination], please
KOKO DESU	Here
ASOKO DESU	Over there
IKURA DESU KA?	How much does it cost?
MOU ICHIDO ONEGAI SHIMASU	Could you repeat that one more time?

SITUATION: SUMMING UP SO FAR

Imagine that you've just gotten out of the airport in Tokyo, and you're riding a train into the city to check in to your hotel. On the way down the steps to the train, the wheel on your luggage broke, and it's quite heavy and hard to carry. You'd rather not carry it in your arms the entire time, and you can't really wheel it anymore. You step out of the train station, and you'd like to hail a cab so that you don't have to carry your luggage all the way to your destination with a broken wheel.

SUMIMASEN!

Excuse me!

A taxi pulls up, and the driver steps out.

NIMOTSU, ONEGAI SHIMASU

Could I trouble you to grab my luggage?

The taxi driver packs your luggage into the trunk, and you get in the car.

KIYOMIZU DERA MADE, ONEGAI SHIMASU

To Kiyomizu temple, please

The driver starts the car, and off you go. As you approach the temple, you see your hotel coming up on the side of the road.

ASOKO MADE, ONEGAI SHIMASU

Just over there is great, thanks

You point to where you'd like for the driver to drop you off.

KOKO DESU!

Right here!

The driver arrives in front of your hotel and stops at the place you indicated. You've made it to your hotel using Japanese!

SITUATION: HOW MUCH IS IT?

You've arrived at your hotel, but there's just one problem—you still need to pay the taxi. While most taxis nowadays have digital displays that will tell you how much you owe, it's best to be prepared to answer this question anyway.

IKURA DESU KA?

How much will it be?

NI SEN EN DESU

2,000 yen

MOU ICHIDO, ONEGAI SHIMASU

Could you repeat that one more time?

NI SEN EN DESU

2,000 yen

KAITE KUDASAI

I'm sorry, could you write that down?

The taxi driver writes down "2,000 円" and hands the paper to you. You pull out a 50,000 yen bill and hand it to him.

OTSURI TO RESHIITO DESU

Here's your change and your receipt

ARIGATOU GOZAIMASU!

Thank you so much!

It's helpful to note that in *otsuri to reshiito, otsuri* means "change," and *reshiito* is borrowed from the English "receipt." The *to* in between means "and"!

Remember that Japan is not entirely fond of credit cards, even in taxis. You'll likely have to pay with cash. Ensure that you're always carrying cash with you in Japan, though it may be wise to break large sums up across multiple pockets or wallets so that should you lose something, you don't lose all your money as well.

SITUATION: A CONVERSATION WITH THE TAXI DRIVER

Depending on where you find yourself in Japan, taxi drivers may be relatively quiet and respectfully leave you to your own devices, or they may be very friendly and try to strike up conversation. While it comes down to personal preference on the part of the taxi driver, areas where tourists are middlingly common but not excessive tend to have the most talkative drivers; they often enjoy figuring out what made you choose this "off the beaten path" option during your travels. One of the most common questions you may be asked in that case is where you come from.

OKUNI WA DOKO DESU KA?

Where are you from?

OKUNI WA DOCHIRA KARA DESU KA?

Which country are you from?

OKUNI WA?

[lit.] What's your country?

The best response to this question is simple (tailored to your specific country, of course):

AMERIKA DESU

I'm from America

WHERE ARE YOU FROM?

It's helpful to make sure you memorize how to pronounce your country in Japanese so that you're ready to answer this question. Many countries' names are nearly identical in Japanese, just adjusted for that language's pronunciation. In the case of Germany, *doitsu* is taken from deutsche.

I'm from...

AMERIKA DESU	America
KANADA DESU	Canada
DOITSU DESU	Germany
OOSUTORARIA DESU	Australia
NYUU JEERANDO DESU	New Zealand
IGIRISU DESU	The UK

Continuing on in the conversation, your Japanese taxi driver might ask some other things.

NIHON WA SUKI DESU KA?

Do you like Japan?

NIHON WA DOU DESU KA?

What do you think of Japan so far?

DAI SUKI DESU!

I love it!

UNDERSTANDING MORE ABOUT TAXIS IN JAPAN

Taxis in Japan are a relatively inexpensive and convenient way to get around, such that even locals may use them from time to time if they don't feel like walking or waiting for a train. In order to get the best value for your taxi, consider traveling with others. In general, a 15-minute ride or 4 to 5 kilometers will cost about 1800 yen, or just shy of $20 USD. If you ride with 4 people, you're looking at just $5 for a taxi ride!

There is often a specific taxi lane out in front of train stations where taxis will park and wait for people who need them. When a taxi driver sees you and acknowledges that he can take you for a ride, pay attention to see if he opens the door for you. Most Japanese taxis have doors that will open and close automatically, so you should let the driver pop the door open for you from the front panel of his car. It is also commonplace, if the taxi is going to be transporting your luggage, to let the taxi driver put it in the trunk. It may seem as though you're trying to be helpful, but in general, drivers prefer that tourists don't interfere too much; putting luggage in the trunk is part of their job, and if their car is going to get scratched up on accident, they'd rather it be *their* accident and not yours.

Drivers will pop open the door for you when you arrive at your destination, and it will often also close on its own. Avoid slamming car doors.

2.5 SHOPPING IN STORES

Japan is a very commercialized country, and you'll find all sorts of stores, from those selling CDs and video games to antiques, memorabilia, and cosmetics—alongside your typical convenience stores, of course.

EXPRESSIONS

KORE KUDASAI	I'll take this, please
KORE HITOTSU KUDASAI	One of this, please
KORE TO KORE TO KORE KUDASAI	This and this and this, please
ARIMASU KA?	Do you have [thing]?
DOKO DESU KA?	Where can I find the [product]?
DAIJOUBU DESU KA?	Is there a problem?

As you may have guessed, *kore* means "this" and will be one of the most useful words you'll learn when it comes to shopping.

SITUATION: LOOKING FOR A FIGURINE

Japan is a country whose pop culture and influence has been felt world-wide. For that reason, especially as you venture into bigger cities, you'll find no shortage of stores catering to these international tastes like anime, video games, and manga. You won't possibly be able to check every store if you're looking for something specific. In this situation, you can whip out your Japanese to cut down your time spent searching and just ask if the store sells what you're looking for.

SUMIMASEN

Excuse me

DORAGON BOORU NO FIGYA, ARIMASU KA?

Do you have Dragon Ball figurines?

DORAGON BOORU NO KOONAA, DOKO DESU KA?

Where is the Dragon Ball section of the store? [lit. where is the Dragon Ball corner?]

CONNECTING WORDS WITH *NO*

Unlike in English, the word *no* in Japanese doesn't mean, well, "no." It makes the same sound, but it's used to make something possessive or descriptive. Put it in between the words that are related to each other and it will connect them.

NARUTO NO TII SHATSU

A Naruto t-shirt

KYOTO NO MACCHA

Green tea from Kyoto

SONII NO KAMERA

A Sony camera

SITUATION: SHOPPING FOR TEA

Imagine that you're in a small boutique looking for a certain kind of tea from the city you're visiting. You can't seem to find what you're looking for.

SUMIMASEN

Excuse me

MACCHA NO KOONAA, DOKO DESU KA?

Where can I find the tea?

A woman leads you to a small shelf with a couple of teas to choose from. After looking them over, you decide on one.

KORE KUDASAI

I'll take this one, please

IKURA DESU KA?

How much is it?

Remember that it's rare to be able to use credit cards in Japan; if you're having trouble counting out your money or understanding the price you're being given, you can always ask *kaite kudasai*, or "could you write that down for me?"

MOU ICHIDO: REPEAT, PLEASE

The expression *mou ichido* will be a common one for tourists. *Ichi* means "one," and *mou* conveys the idea of "again"—thus, "once again," or "one more time."

MOU ICHIDO, ONEGAI SHIMASU
One more time, please

KAITE KUDASAI, SUMIMASEN
I'm sorry, could you write that down please?

SITUATION: UNDERSTANDING WHAT'S ALLOWED

As a tourist in Japan, you're often going to be faced with situations that you don't know how to handle because you've never been there before. Are you allowed to bring food into the temple? Can you take pictures?

SUMIMASEN
Excuse me

SHICHAKU, DAIJOUBU DESU KA?
Could I try these clothes on?

FOTO, DAIJOUBU DESU KA?
Is taking pictures allowed?

MITEMO DAIJOUBU DESU KA?
Is it okay to take a look?

SAWATTEMO DAIJOUBU DESU KA?
Can I sit here?

ASKING FOR PERMISSION IN JAPANESE

The expression *daijoubu desu ka* is used with nearly as much frequency in Japan as *sumimasen*, one of the most common phrases of all time. Its meaning is similar to "is that okay" or "is that allowed?"

DAIJOUBU DESU KA

The phrase *daijoubu desu ka* can be attached to quite a number of words to form a phrase meaning, essentially, "is there a problem with [thing]?"

TABAKO DAIJOUBU DESU KA?
Is smoking okay?

OSAKE DAIJOUBU DESU KA?
Can I drink?

Osake is the word for all alcohol, not just sake. In reference specifically to sake as a beverage (distilled rice wine), Japanese people will use the term *nihon shu*.

MITEMO DAIJOUBU DESU KA?
Can I look?

HAITTEMO DAIJOUBU DESU KA?
Is it okay to go inside?

SAWATTEMO DAIJOUBU DESU KA?
May I sit?

Mitemo, haittemo, and *sawattemo* are verbs that have been conjugated from *miru*, *hairu*, and *sawaru*, respectively. They mean to see, to enter, and to sit.

SITUATION: ADJECTIVES WHEN TRYING ON CLOTHES

Imagine that you're at a store, and you've found a line of clothing that you would really like to try on. Using some adjectives, you can convey the information needed to make sure you find the right size.

OKKII NO ARIMASU KA?

Do you have a large one?

MOTTO OKKII NO ARIMASU KA?

Do you have a bigger one?

CHICHAI NO ARIMASU KA?

Do you have a small one?

MOTTO CHICHAI NO ARIMASU KA?

Do you have a smaller one?

SUMIMASEN, SAIZU AWANAI DESU

Sorry, this size isn't right/doesn't fit

ABOUT SIZES AND COLORS

Basic adjectives can really come in handy as you navigate through Japan as a tourist, so spend some time memorizing them and getting to know what they mean so that you'll have them ready at your disposal.

MEMORIZING VOCAB

Here are some of the most common color words you'll need.

KURO black

SHIRO white

AKA red

AO blue or green

PINKU pink

KIIRO yellow

As for sizing, you have:

MOTTO more

CHICHAI small

OKKII large

These words can be used with common expressions to explain your meaning.

ARIMASU KA? Do you have?

SAISU Size (taken from English)

AWANAI DESU Doesn't fit

EXERCISE: PRACTICING COLOR AND SIZING

Imagine that you're at a store and would like to try on some new clothes. Visualize everything you'll need to say, and then practice with yourself using the following template as a guide.

OKKII NO ARIMASU KA?

Do you have a large?

MOTTO OKKII NO ARIMASU KA?

Do you have a larger size?

____

Do you have a red one? A black one? A pink one?

____

Do you have a blue one? A white one?

____

This size doesn't fit me

____

Do you have a smaller one?

SITUATION: REACTING TO REALITY

As with many things in life, you'll encounter situations in Japan about which you have an opinion. This might be while shopping or even just when interacting with friends.

YASUI DESU NE!

Wow, that's cheap!

TAKAI DESU NE!

That's expensive!

In general, if something takes you by surprise, *sugoi* or "incredible" is a good choice.

SUGOI DESU NE

Wow, amazing

SITUATION: PAYING WITH CASH OR CARD

At least about 60% of transactions in Japan use coins and bills, not credit cards. This will vary from city to city and even from market niche to niche, but in general, it's safest to plan on not using a card at all, though you may still bring one for safety's sake. If a purchase is large or you've run out of cash, you may need to ask if it's all right to pay with a card.

SUMIMASEN

Excuse me

CREDIT CARD OK DESU KA?

Is a credit card okay?

CREDIT CARD DAIJOUBU DESU KA?

Is it all right to pay with a credit card?

SUMIMASEN, GENKIN DAKE

Sorry, we only accept cash

SUMIMASEN, GENKIN NOMI

Sorry, it's cash only

THE THIRD FORM OF "IS IT OKAY?"

Japanese contains essentially three methods by which to say "can I?" You have already learned two so far:

OK DESU KA?

Is that okay?

DAIJOUBU DESU KA?

Is that okay?

The third form of this phrasing comes from *tsukau*, the verb meaning "to use."

TSUKAEMASU KA?

Can I use that?

CREDIT CARD TSUKAEMASU KA?

Is it okay if I use a credit card?

The difference between the three methods comes down to a slight variation in meaning. While *OK* and *daijoubu* both mean "all right," *tsukaemasu* specifically means "able to use." So you'll only be able to use *tsukaemasu ka* in the context of something you're allowed to *use*, not something you're allowed to *do*. If you want to ask if you can use a bench, *tsukaemasu* is fine. If you want to ask if you can sit down, you'll have to choose one of the other two.

CREDIT CARD OK DESU KA?

Is a credit card ok?

CREDIT CARD DAIJOUBU DESU KA?

Is a credit card all right?

CREDIT CARD TSUKAEMASU KA?

Can I use a credit card?

EXERCISE: USING "OK" AND "CAN I?"

Take a minute to practice using these three phrases.

[SOMETHING] OK DESU KA?

[SOMETHING] DAIJOUBU DESU KA?

[SOMETHING] TSUKAEMASU KA?

Take a look at the following useful words and consider whether they might pair with some or all of the phrases above.

BISA KAADO	Credit card [lit. Visa card]
DEBITTO KAADO	Debit card
JR PASS	JR Pass
KORE	This
______________	A vocabulary word of your choice
______________	
______________	
______________	

2.6 IN THE CAFÉ AND CAFETERIA

In Japan, you'll find two different types of cafés: *kissaten* and more modern cafés (simply called *kafe*) like Starbucks. While there is a difference between them in terms of the products that they serve and the atmosphere you'll find, in general, your usage of Japanese is going to be the same regardless of which you choose.

Kissaten are more historical "cafés"; you might even think of them as teahouses or coffee houses. They originate from the Meiji, Taisho, and Showa eras (from 1868 to 1989).

In a *kissaten*, expect to find much more traditional offerings, like green tea, local specialty tea, or coffee without very much modification (no mochas and the like). The historic atmosphere of a *kissaten* often draws tourists, so you may find yourself in one sooner than you expect. Their architecture and design can be appealing both visually and spatially, making many of them—and especially some of the older ones in places like Kyoto—very worthwhile to visit.

The other type of *kafe*, which is like Starbucks, will include a number of global brands of tea and coffee companies that you're probably a lot more used to. You'll find these everywhere, including airports, and their menus will be full of creative and appealing drinks that might change by season or special event. Japan is notorious for some of its unique flavors at these restaurants; you might find taro shakes (a kind of purplish potato-like vegetable that's sweeter than you'd expect), macha, and durian-flavored drinks.

PHRASES YOU'LL HEAR

Sometimes, the challenge you'll face as a tourist in Japan isn't with speaking Japanese but rather understanding what's being spoken to you.

GOCHUUMON WA OKIMARI DESU KA?

Have you decided on what to order?

OKAIKEI WA NANA HYAKU EN DESU

Your bill comes to 700 yen

PHRASES TO USE

In a *kissaten*, the things that you ask might be slightly different than your standard order in a *kafe*. Take a look at these phrases and see if you can tell which you're more likely to use in each situation.

HITOTSU, ONEGAI SHIMASU
Just one, please

KAFE LATE, HOTTO, EM SAIZU
One café latte, hot, size medium, please

OSUSUME, NAN DESU KA?
What do you recommend?

OMIZU ARIMASU KA?
Could I get some water?

OKAIKE, BETSU BETSU DE, ONEGAI SHIMASU
Could we please split the bill and pay separately?

SITUATION: NO ENGLISH MENU IN THE KISSATEN

Imagine that a beautiful *kissaten* has caught your eye, and you'd like to go inside. Upon entering, you notice that they are only displaying a Japanese menu. You'd really like to try out some of the coffee, but you're worried about not having an English menu to look at.

IRASSHAIMASE!
Welcome to our coffee shop!

GOCHUUMON WA OKIMARI DESU KA?
Do you know what you'd like to order?

EIGO NO MENYUU, ARIMASU KA?
Do you have an English menu?

SUMIMASEN, ARIMASEN

I'm sorry, we don't

KOOHII ARIMASU KA?

Do you have coffee?

HAI, ARIMASU

Yes, we do!

KOOHII, FUTATSU KUDASAI

We'll take two coffees then, please!

SITUATION: A DIFFERENT MENU

What happens if you enter a place that *does* have an English menu, but once they bring it to you, you find it has no Japanese on it at all? You'll have to remember how to say a couple of things if you'd like to order in Japanese.

IRASSHAIMASE!

Welcome!

GOCHUUMON WA OKIMARI DESU KA?

Have you decided on your order?

EIGO NO MENU ARIMASU KA?

Do you have an English menu?

HAI, DOUZO

Yes, here you go

KEEKI SETTO FUTATSU, ONEGAI SHIMASU

We'll take two of the cake sets, please

KOOHII KA KOUCHA DESU KA?

Would you like coffee or black tea?

HOTTO KOOHII, ONEGAI SHIMASU

Coffee, please

TIPS FOR CAFÉS IN JAPAN

In general, you'll find that cafés in Japan are largely like their American and European counterparts. A service worker will take your order, and the items you order will often be essentially equivalent to the products you're used to. In fact, Japanese borrows many coffee-related terms from English (or their language of origin, if not English).

HOTTO KOOHII, ONEGAI SHIMASU

One hot coffee, please [hotto koohii = hot coffee]

AISU KOOHII, ONEGAI SHIMASU

I'll take an iced coffee, please [aisu koohii = ice coffee]

SITUATION: PAYING AT A CAFÉ

As discussed previously, there is no guarantee that a store or business you go to in Japan will take credit cards, but this is especially true of traditional cafés. It is very common for a *kissaten* to only accept bills and coins. Thus, the server may only speak the bill to you rather than give you a paper copy.

OKAIKEI ONEGAI SHIMASU

Could I have the bill, please?

OKAIKEI WA NANA HYAKU EN DESU

That will be 700 yen

KAITE KUDASAI, SUMIMASEN

I'm sorry, could you write that down for me?

KUREJITTO KAADO, OK DESU KA?

Is a credit card okay?

SUMIMASEN, GENKIN DAKE DESU

I'm sorry, we only take cash

SITUATION: A MODERN CAFÉ

If you're going to frequent a more modern café like Starbucks, you'll have a lot more options for what to order. This might bring up some new phrases for you as the server repeats back your order.

GOCHUUMON WA OKIMARI DESU KA?

Have you decided on your order?

KAFE LATE, HOTTO, EM SAIZU HITOTSU, ONEGAI SHIMASU

I'll take one medium-sized hot café latte

SOREKARA, DOONATSU HITOTSU, ONEGAI SHIMASU

Oh also, one donut, please

DOONATSU HITOTSU DE, KAFE LATE HOTTO EM SAIZU HITOTSU DESU

So that's one donut and one medium hot café latte

SOCHIRA DE, OMACHI KUDASAI

All right, please wait for just a moment!

OKAIKEI WA NANA HYAKU EN DESU

Your total will be 700 yen

KUREJITTO KAADO, OK DESU KA?

Is it okay to use a credit card?

SUMIMASEN, GENKIN DAKE DESU

I'm sorry, we only take cash

SITUATION: LOOKING FOR A RECOMMENDATION

Imagine that you enter a café but find that they don't have an English menu, and their Japanese menu is made up of kanji you can't read without pictures of any of the items for sale. In this situation, it can be helpful to ask for a recommendation.

SUMIMASEN

Excuse me

OSUSUME NAN DESU KA?

What do you recommend from the menu?

OSUSUME, ARIMASU KA?

Do you have any recommendations?

KONO KEEKI SETTO WA OSUSUME DESU

I'd recommend this cake set

KORE KUDASAI

I'll take this!

OHITOTSU? OFUTATSU DESU KA?

Just one? Two?

KORE HITOTSU, KORE HITOTSU, ONEGAI SHIMASU

I'll take one of these and one of these, please

You may notice that you've already learned the words *hitotsu* and *futatsu* before, but in this example, the server is using *ohitotsu* and *ofutatsu*, with an "o" in front, instead. This is the server's way of being formal with you, and it's the same reason that asking how someone is doing is *ogenki desu ka* instead of simply *genki desu ka*. The "o" adds respect when asking these questions. You do not need to worry about doing this on your own. The phrases you've learned in this guide are all formal enough to be polite without any further modification.

SITUATION: COLD WATER FOR TWO

Is cold water free in Japanese restaurants and cafés? Many tourists find themselves wondering that the first time they spend a day out on the town in the middle of spring or summer—the most common tourist times—and discover that the humidity and heat really knock the wind out of their sails.

One of the nicest things about almost all restaurants, cafés, and other eateries in Japan is that they will provide water to customers who ask free of charge. If you're traveling and need to take a break for a drink, don't hesitate to stop in and ask for some water.

SUMIMASEN

Excuse me

OMIZU ARIMASU KA?

Do you have any water?

OMIZU KUDASAI

I'll take some water, please

SITUATION: ASKING FOR WATER

Previously, this book has lightly touched on being able to count out the number of things you'd like to order. This will become particularly useful in this context, when you're stopping in somewhere to ask for water with your order.

OMIZU, HITOTSU KUDASAI

One water please

OMIZU, FUTATSU KUDASAI

Two waters please

OMIZU, MITSU KUDASAI

Three waters, please

If it's a particularly hot day out, you may find that just one glass of water isn't enough. In this case, it's easy to ask for a refill.

OMIZU NO OKAWARI, IKAGA DESU KA?

Could I have a refill of my water, please?

HAI, SUMIMASEN!

Sure, sorry about that!

Okawari means "in exchange" or "a replacement." It works with more than just water, but understand that the concept of "free refills" is largely an American idea. If you ask for refills of anything besides water (and possibly tea), you'll likely be charged as if you had ordered it like normal.

OMIZU NO OKAWARI, KUDASAI!

One water refill, please!

SITUATION: PAYING FOR THINGS SEPARATELY

It's likely that you'll be eating with friends in Japan, if not during the entire trip, then at least for a meal or two. Assuming that your friends aren't planning on paying for your meal (or that you aren't treating your friends all the time), you'll need to eventually ask to split the bill after your table has finished eating.

OKAIKEI WA GOISSHO DESU KA?

And is this bill all together?

OKAIKEI, BETSU BETSU DE, ONEGAI SHIMASU

Could we have the bill separately, please?

OKAIKEI ISSHO DE ONEGAI SHIMASU

Could we have just one bill for all of us, please?

GOCHISOUSAMA DESHITA

Thanks for the food!

ARIGATOU GOZAIMASHITA!

Thank you!

2.7 ORDERING IN A RESTAURANT

You'll find no shortage of restaurants in Japan to please just about any taste and style of dining. Traditional Japanese restaurants tend to be rather small, fitting only around 10 people at a time. Conversely, family restaurants are more suited to larger numbers and may have more global menu choices. At many traditional restaurants, you'll have your choice of at least some of the Japanese classics—sushi, sashimi, okonomiyaki, takoyaki, or a variety of grilled and seared meat like yakiniku.

It can be a little unclear what some of these "classic" Japanese dishes are, so take it from the perspective of a non-native.

Sushi: This refers to both *nigiri* and *maki*. Nigiri are the pieces of fish that are draped over a strip of rice. Maki are the rolls most English speakers are familiar with.

Sashimi: This is just fish, no rice. It may also include other individual cuts like eel, shrimp, octopus, and similar. Such things as dessert sashimi (made with a strip of sweet egg) also exist.

Okonomiyaki: This is a cabbage dish that sort of comes together almost like a savory pancake. If you opt to get one from Hiroshima in particular, the local variety has noodles in it too!

Takoyaki: These are balls of octopus. They may not sound appetizing, but they're a bit like calamari, if the calamari wasn't coated in something crunchy on the outside but rather something soft and batter-like.

If you're searching for family restaurants with food you're more familiar with, some common chains like Denny's and McDonald's have a substantial presence in Japan. You'll be able to find these options without searching too far, so you'll always have something you know you'll be able to enjoy. That being said, few things are better than trying local Japanese food!

EXPRESSIONS

HITORI DESU	It's just me (when speaking about party size)
ONEGAI SHIMASU	Please
KARAI DESU KA?	Is this spicy?
OSUSUME	Recommendation
TEISHOKU	The menu of the day
NASHI DE	Without (when trying to remove something from order)
HAITTEIMASU KA	Can I come in?

How much Japanese you'll need to use depends on where you're traveling to. In Tokyo, many service workers speak at least some English, so you might not even need Japanese in order to place your order.

SITUATION: ENTERING A RESTAURANT

By this point, you're probably already familiar with some of the things that servers will say to you when you enter a restaurant, like *irasshaimase*. However, you might be asked a couple extra questions too.

IRASSHAIMASE!

Welcome!

NANMEI SAMA DESU KA?

How many in your party?

SUMIMASEN, HITORI DESU

Oh, it's just me

OTABAKO WA?

Smoking or non-smoking?

NO SMOKING DE ONEGAI SHIMASU

Non-smoking, please

HAI, OMACHI KUDASAI!

Sure, please wait just a moment

KOCHIRA HE DOUZO

You can follow me/this way

When announcing how many are in your party, remember this:

HITORI = 1

FUTARI = 2

For anything above this, you can put together the word by combining the correct number with the word for person, "nin."

SANNIN = 3

YONIN = 4

GONIN = 5

ROKUNIN = 6

And so on.

SITUATION: ORDERING SPECIALTY CUISINE

Sometimes, whether because of personal beliefs, allergies, or preferences, you might want to make a special order or tailor your meal to suit you. You can use the word *desu*, which means "is" or "am," to explain your situation.

BEJITARIAN DESU

I'm vegetarian

ARERUGI DESU

I have allergies [lit. [the reason I will not eat this] is allergies]

Similarly, you can ask for your meal to be prepared without certain ingredients, but understand that complicated substitutions are not common in Japan; in general, you're expected to eat the meal as it's normally prepared.

WASABI NASHI DE ONEGAI SHIMASU

Could I have this without wasabi, please?

TAMAGO NASHI DE ONEGAI SHIMASU

No egg, please

WASABI HAITTE IMASU KA?

Does this have wasabi in it?

KOMUGIKO HAITTE IMASU KA?

Is this made with wheat?

PROBLEMATIC INGREDIENTS

WASABI	wasabi
NINNIKU	garlic
TAMANEGI	onion
NEGI	onion (green)
TAMAGO	egg
NATTSU	nuts
KOMUGIKO	wheat
GYUUNYUU	milk

EXERCISE: PRACTICING THE MENU

Depending on where you choose to eat, you may encounter a "meal of the day" or meal set that is specific for one day of the week. This is called a *teishoku*.

HAMBAAGU TEISHOKU	Hamburger meal set
KARAAGE TEISHOKU	Fried chicken meal set
PASTA TEISHOKU	Pasta meal set

SITUATION: RESTAURANT EATING

By this point, you have all the tools you need to carry on a full conversation in a restaurant, whether you're by yourself or with a party, paying with card or cash.

OKAIKEI ONEGAI SHIMASU

The check, please

OKAIKEI WA GOISSHO DESU KA?

And will that be all together?

OKAIKEI, BETSU BETSU DE, ONEGAI SHIMASU

We'll take separate checks

OKAIKEI, ISSHO DE ONEGAI SHIMASU

We're all together

CREDIT CARD OK DESU KA?

Can I pay with a credit card?

GOCHISOU SAMA DESHITA!

It was delicious!

Gochisou sama deshita is a polite turn of phrase meaning "that meal was a delicacy, thank you for serving it!" or "I'm grateful to have eaten this." *Gochisou* means "a great delicacy," and so the phrase comes across as "what an awesome meal!"

ASKING FOR SEPARATE CHECKS

This book has already covered the ways to clarify how you want the check to be split (or not) while you're out eating. The reason these phrases work comes down to three words: *issho* and *betsu betsu*. *Issho* means "together," and *betsu betsu* means "separate" or "in pieces."

OKAIKEI, BETSU BETSU DE, ONEGAI SHIMASU

Could we please split the check?

OKAIKEI, ISSHO DE ONEGAI SHIMASU

We're all on one bill

2.8 WHEN ORDERING AT A BAR

In Japan, there are essentially two different types of bars:

- Omise: A more classic, almost club-like environment; technically hostess clubs and the like fit in this category as well.
- Izakaya: A favorite of Japanese salarymen, this is a location where a small featured menu is provided alongside drinks, and tables are organized such that you often sit together with a group in a large booth

IMPORTANT PHRASES: I'D LIKE A BEER

NAMA BIIRU, IPPAI!
A draft beer, please!

NAMA BIIRU, HITOTSU KUDASAI!
One draft beer, please!

The more natural form of expression here is using *ippai*, but *hitotsu* is also understandable and should already be at least a little bit practiced from all the other opportunities you'll have to use it. *Kudasai*, of course, indicates "please" and ensures that your request remains polite—even if you're getting a little bit tipsy.

EXERCISE: PRACTICING YOUR ORDER

Learning all the options on an izakaya menu is a great opportunity to practice *kudasai* as well. Try to form complete sentences to order each of these drinks using the following template:

[DRINK] HITOTSU KUDASAI!
One [drink] please!

NAMA BIIRU	draft beer
HIGH BALL	whiskey soda
UISKII	whiskey
NIHON SHU	Japanese sake
SOFTO DORINKU	soft drink
KORE	this

SITUATION: BEING SERVED AT A BAR

Like any other restaurant or place of service, expect to be greeted at a bar as soon as you enter. You'll still be met with the same questions about being ready to order, but they may come in a slightly different form, under the expectation that you won't just be ordering one drink and leaving.

***IRASSHAI*!**

Welcome! [this is a more casual form of *irasshaimase*]

GOCHUUMON WA OKIMARI DESU KA?

Do you know what you'd like to order?

TORIAEZU, BIIRU

Let's start with a beer

HITOTSU?

One?

HAI, HITOTSU KUDASAI!

Yep, just one please!

Toriaezu means "at the moment" and indicates that you'll likely be ordering more. Think of it like saying "I'll start with a beer" or "I'll take one beer for now, but maybe I'll think of something else I'd like later." It can also mean "first of all."

SITUATION: ORDERING MULTIPLE DRINKS

You might go out to drink by yourself—some people really enjoy that—but odds are that you'll end up going to a bar with more than one person. If that's the case, you'll need to know how to wrap your order together; thankfully, you've already had some practice with this.

HITOTSU	one
FUTATSU	two
MITSU	three
KUDASAI	please

IRASSHAI!

Welcome!

GOCHUUMON WA OKIMARI DESU KA?

Have you decided on your order?

HAI! NAMA BIIRU FUTATSU KUDASAI.
HIGH BALL HITOTSU KUDASAI.

Yes! Two draft beers and one high ball, please.

HAI, OMACHI KUDASAI!

Sure, please wait just a moment!

SITUATION: ASKING FOR A MENU IN ENGLISH

Some bars will have a lot of alcoholic or food options that you might not recognize, and in that case, it would be nice to have an English menu on which you can browse the options.

EIGO NO MENYUU ARIMASU KA?

Do you have an English menu?

HAI, ARIMASU! OMOCHI SHIMASU

Yes, we do! I'll bring it for you

KORE HITOTSU KUDASAI

I'll have one of these, please

KORE FUTATSU KUDASAI

I'll have two of these, please

KORE MITSU KUDASAI

Three of these, please

SUMIMASEN

Sorry about the hassle (thanks)

SITUATION: WHAT TO DO WHEN THERE'S NO ENGLISH MENU

It can be challenging to arrive in a bar only to find that there's no English menu, the current menu is mainly in kanji, or that there are no pictures to help with ordering. In this case, asking the server some basic questions or what they recommend can go a long way

OSUSUME, NAN DESU KA?

What's your recommendation?

KORE NAN DESU KA?

What's this?

KARAI DESU KA?

Is this spicy?

WHISKEY ARIMASU KA?

Do you have whiskey?

SITUATION: WASABI IN A MEAL

Some izakaya foods in particular are specialty dishes that not everyone will enjoy, so it's often a good idea to ask what's in the food you order. For more specifics, refer back to 2.7.

KORE NAN DESU KA?
What is this?

TAKOWASA DESU
It's takowasa

WASABI HAITTE IMASU KA?
Is there wasabi in it?

HAI, WASABI HAITTE IMASU
Yes, it has wasabi

WASABI NUKI DE ONEGAI SHIMASU
I'll take it without wasabi, please

EXERCISE: BAR FOOD

Imagine the situation: you've sat down at an izakaya with your friends, and you're looking to snack throughout the night as you enjoy some drinks. The menu has a couple items you don't recognize.

KARAAGE	fried chicken
TEMPURA MORIAWASE	A variety of floured fried vegetables
EBI FURAI	fried shrimp
NANKOTSU	cartilage
EDAMAME	cooked soy beans
UINNAA	weiners (small Vienna sausages)
TSUKUNE	a sort of chicken meatball

2.9 MAKING PURCHASES IN A CONVENIENCE STORE

One of the most common establishments you're sure to encounter in Japan is the convenience store. The country boasts more than 60,000 such stores, the most famous being 7-Eleven, Family Mart, and Lawson. You'll often see students working at these establishments part-time to earn income, so the staff tend to be younger.

Many tourists who are new to Japan are surprised at both the quality and quantity of items you can find in a convenience store. In fact, many people's favorite meals come from a conbini! This is not a place to find low-quality bags of potato chips; you can find entire prepare meals like curry, fresh items, and a wide variety of drinks and snacks.

EXPRESSIONS

SUMIMASEN	Excuse me
ONEGAI SHIMASU	Please
HITOTSU KUDASAI	One please
IRIMASEN	No thanks
DAIJOUBU DESU	That's good/OK
ATATAMEMASU KA?	Shall I warm that up for you?
FUKURO WA YOROSHII DESU KA?	Would you like a bag?

SITUATION: BUYING A BENTO

Imagine that you're in a convenience store, and you notice a tasty-looking box of food. This is called a *bento*, and it's a common lunch staple. You choose to buy one and head up to the counter to complete your purchase.

SUMIMASEN

Excuse me

OKAIKEE WA ROPPYAKU HACHIJYUU EN DESU

That'll be 680 yen

FUKURO WA GORIYOU DESU KA?

Do you need a bag?

IRIMASEN

No thanks

ATATAMEMASU KA?

Would you like me to heat this up?

HAI

Yes please

POINTO KAADO WA OMOCHI DESU KA?

Do you have a point card/loyalty card for the store?

IRIMASEN

No I don't, thanks

RESHIITO WA IRIMASU KA?

Do you need a receipt?

ONEGAI SHIMASU

Yes please

IRIMASEN = DON'T NEED

As you may have been able to gather from the previous exercise, *irimasen* means "don't need." However, it can also mean "no thank you" in the sense of someone offering you something. For example, if a cashier asks about whether you have a point card, *irimasen* conveys both "no I don't" and "I'm not interested in signing up for one right now, thanks."

ONEGAI SHIMASU = YES PLEASE

Remember that "please" is often best conveyed as *onegai shimasu*. *Onegai* means "a favor," so the phrase more closely means "if you'd be so kind as to do that favor for me."

WHAT TO DO AT A CONVENIENCE STORE

You can do much more at a convenience store than just buy snacks in Japan!

- Withdraw money and use an ATM
- Eat in with some convenience stores' dollar menus
- Buy some snacks for later; one of the classics is *melonpan*, a melon-flavored bread covered in a cookie crust
- Stop by midday for a lunch box (*bento*) you can carry with you for later
- Buy a variety of drinks, including alcohol and coffee, as well as freshly made fried food
- Make use of free public toilet access
- Read or buy manga; it's not uncommon for people to stand in a convenience store reading manga instead of buying it

SITUATION: SPENDING 100 YEN AT THE CONVENIENCE STORE

The convenience store is one of the most common places to find the drink you're craving in the morning, since these businesses have such a large variety available.

SUMIMASEN

Excuse me

HOTTO KOOHII, REGYURAA, HITOTSU KUDASAI

One regular hot coffee, please

HOTTO, REGYURAA DESU NE

A regular hot coffee, yes?

OKAIKEI WA HYAKU EN DESU

That'll be 100 yen

POINTO KAADO WA OMOCHI DESU KA?

Do you have a point card?

IRIMASEN

No, thanks

WORDING YOUR ORDER

Whether you're placing an order at 7-Eleven, Family Mart, or Lawson, the best order to phrase your request in is this:

NAME	SIZE	NUMBER	PLEASE
HOTTO KOOHII	REGYURAA	HITOTSU	KUDASAI
KAFE LATE	EERU SAIZU	FUTATSU	KUDASAI

HOTTO KOOHII REGYURAA HITOTSU KUDASAI

One regular hot coffee, please

KAFE LATE EERU SAIZU FUTATSU KUDASAI

Two L-size (large) café lattes, please

CORRECTING YOUR ORDER

Sometimes, you might make a mistake while ordering, or you might notice something you'd rather have after you order. In these situations, you can quickly change your order if you ask nicely.

A! SUMIMASEN! HOTTO KOOHII IRIMASEN

Oh! Sorry! I don't need that hot coffee

KAFE LATE HITOTSU KUDASAI

I'll take one café latte

SORE TO, AISU KOOHII, REGYURAA, HITOTSU KUDASAI

I'll also add one regular iced coffee, please

KAIKEI WA NIHYAKU GOJYUU EN DESU

That'll be 250 yen

MOST COMMON TYPES OF COFFEE

Japan has a couple very common forms of coffee; if you're looking for rarer varieties like coffee with alcohol, you'll likely need to go to a specialized coffee shop.

HOTTO KOOHII

From the English "hot coffee," this is just your standard hot beverage.

AISU KOOHII

From the English "ice coffee," this will be an iced coffee, usually with large ice cubes (which sometimes come in cute shapes).

KAFE LATE

Like its foreign derivative "café latte," this is coffee with milk.

KAFE MOKA

From the phonetic "café mocha," this coffee contains both milk and chocolate.

2.10 ORIENTING YOURSELF IN THE TRAIN STATION

Japan is famous around the world for its exceptional railway system that connects the bustling country conveniently, affordably, and quickly. Japan Railways (JR) is the predominant travel group, and you'll see more than just trains working under the JR umbrella. You'll also likely at least consider purchasing a JR Pass, which gives you unlimited access to all JR transport in Japan.

Because trains are such a ubiquitous way to get around in Japan, stations tend to be clearly labeled, and finding the train you need is relatively easy. The signs on each platform will show a couple of important pieces of information. In the center of the sign will be the name of the station you're currently at. The sign will also likely have a colored stripe that indicates which train line you're standing on. It may just be a color (for example, bright green in Tokyo means the Yamanote line). On the sides of the sign will be the previous and next train stations (for small stations) or the "landmark" or end stations in each direction (for large stations). So look at a map, take note of which direction your stop is (pay attention to the next station name, as well as the station at the end of the line in that direction), and then stand on the side that displays one of those station names. The train on the opposite side of the platform will be going the opposite way.

If you have a JR pass or other travel pass, you won't be able to go through the ticket scanners. *Never* attempt to insert your pass into a ticket scanner. Instead, find the large glass booth off to one side of the row of ticket gates and show your pass to the attendant inside. If you can't find this booth, search the station for a picture of a station attendant holding up one arm and then follow those signs. You usually do not even need to say anything to the attendant; they will likely just wave you on as soon as they see your pass.

If you get lost and need help figuring out where to go next, these same people in the glass booths are also the ones you can ask for help.

EXPRESSIONS

DOKO DESU KA?

Where is [x]/where am I?

USJ NI IKITAI DESU

I'd like to go to USJ

USJ DE TOMARIMASU KA?

Does this make a stop at USJ?

NORIKAE ARIMASU KA?

Is there a transfer?

WASUREMONO DESU

You forgot something!

SITUATION: AT THE STATION

Imagine that you've been planning to go to Universal Studios Japan (USJ) for some time now, and you're heading out to visit. You get to the station, and you realize that you're not sure which train will take you there. You stop by the information desk to ask.

SUMIMASEN

Excuse me

USJ NI IKITAI DESU

I'd like to go to USJ

ICHIBAN HOOMU DESU

Platform 1 [is where you should go]

NORIKAE ARIMASU KA?

Will there be a transfer?

HAI! NISHIKUJOU DESU. NISHIKUJOU DE NIBAN HOOMU DESU

Yes! It's at Nishikujou. At Nishikujou, go to platform 2

ARIGATOU GOZAIMASU

Thanks so much!

Hoomu means "platform," and *norikae* means "transfer."

PLATFORM NUMBERS

Like most other ways of counting, platforms also have their own counter. You can count platforms by using your regular numbers + *ban*.

ICHIBAN HOOMU	platform 1
NIBAN HOOMU	platform 2
SANBAN HOOMU	platform 3
YONBAN HOOMU	platform 4

SITUATION: ASKING ABOUT A TRAIN

In many train stations, especially in busier cities, you'll often see train attendants walking on the platforms greeting the trains and waving them on. You may also occasionally see the train driver leaning out the window. All of these people will be happy to help you if you have questions about a particular train; don't hesitate to stop them to ask a question.

SUMIMASEN

Excuse me

KORE, NANBA NI IKIMASU KA?

Does this [train] go to Nanba?

HAI, IKIMASU

Yes, it does

KORE, NANBA DE TOMARIMASU KA?

Does this [train] stop at Nanba?

HAI, TOMARIMASU

Yes, it does

NORIKAE, ARIMASU KA?

Is there a transfer?

ARIMASEN

No, no transfer

ARIGATOU GOZAIMASU

Thanks so much!

The phrases *ikimasu ka* (“go to?”) and *tomarimasu ka* (“stop at?”) will be very helpful to you as you travel throughout Japan.

EXPRESSIONS “STOP AT” AND “GO TO”

The two most important verbs you’ll need to have a handle on when traveling in Japan are “stop at” and “go to.”

TOMARIMASU KA? / STOP AT?

IKIMASU KA? / GO TO?

Tomarimasu uses the particle *de*; in other words, always put *de* before *tomarimasu*.

OSAKA DE TOMARIMASU KA?

Does this stop at Osaka?

Ikimasu uses the particle *ni*; in other words, always put *ni* before *ikimasu*.

KOBE NI IKIMASU KA?

Does this go to Kobe?

SITUATION: ASKING ABOUT YOUR TRAIN JOURNEY

Sometimes, rail travel in Japan can become more complicated. This is mostly the case if you’ll be switching from JR to a local line that’s not part of the JR network. In these situations, it’s best to confirm with a station attendant what you’re supposed to do.

SUMIMASEN

Excuse me

KORE OSAKA NI IKIMASU KA?

Does this train go to Osaka?

HAI, IKIMASU!

Yes it does go there!

NORIKAE ARIMASU KA?

Is there a transfer?

HAI, SHIN-OSAKA DE NORIKAE DESU. 2 (NI) BAN HOOMU DESU

Yes, there's a transfer in Shin-Osaka. It's on platform 2.

It's also important to note, regarding switching from JR lines to local lines, that your JR Pass will likely not work anymore (unless you're on a couple very specific railways). You'll need to buy new tickets, which you can do at ticket machines. These machines are set up so that you must click on the name of the station you're going to. On one side of the screen will be pictures of people; select the picture that corresponds to how many people you're buying tickets for. Be sure to pick up your tickets when they come out of the machine; you'll need to use them both to get through the ticket gate and also to get out on the other side.

SITUATION: YOU'VE ACCIDENTALLY DROPPED SOMETHING

Imagine that you're at a train station and notice that your wallet has gone missing. Did you leave it on the last train? Did it fall out of your pocket? In this situation, it's best to go to the Lost and Found (*wasuremono sentaa*, lit. "forgotten things center") to see if it's been dropped off.

SUMIMASEN

Excuse me

DENSHA DE WASUREMONO DESU!

I left something on the train!

WASUREMONO SENTAA, DOKO DESU KA?

Where's the Lost and Found?

EIGO DAIJOUBU DESU KA?

Is English okay (i.e., "can we speak in English?")

EIGO DE ONEGAI SHIMASU

In English, please

EXERCISE: I'VE LOST MY PASSPORT!

In Japan, one of the most important possessions you'll be carrying is your passport. And since you'll be out in public and on transit quite a bit, odds are you'll likely leave something behind somewhere at some point. If you've ever left anything behind, head on over to a Lost and Found.

PASPOOTO, WASUREMASHITA!

I forgot my passport!

MORE USEFUL INFORMATION ABOUT TRAINS

In Japan, trains are *extremely* timely. If a train says it will arrive at 3:13, it will arrive at 3:13; not 3:12, not 3:14. Keep this in mind when preparing to board a train, as it will likely not be there if you're running late.

The fastest trains in Japan are the *shinkansen*, and depending on what type of ticket you have, you may or may not be allowed to ride one. You'll have to purchase a ticket from a special office, and even JR Pass holders who are allowed to ride some shinkansen aren't allowed to ride the fastest variants, like Nozomi. These trains, while more expensive than standard JR lines, are highly recommended to pass through large sections of Japan quickly. You can cover the entire country in just a couple hours.

Even if you hold a JR Pass and are permitted to ride the "slower" shinkansen like Kodama and Hikari, *do not* simply board the shinkansen with your JR Pass. You still need to stop by the shinkansen ticket office and get a paper ticket. It will be free because of the JR Pass, but you still need the small ticket in order to pass through the gate and not get in trouble. Shinkansen tickets can be scheduled, so you may want to consider this if you're going to be traveling during peak times or are afraid of missing your train. Be aware that there may be lines for shinkansen tickets at certain times of day, as businessmen tend to have long commutes that necessitate these trains.

If you want to ride a shinkansen but are late in buying a ticket, you may still be able to get on in non-reserved seating, which is on a first come, first served basis. There is also usually some standing room, if you're willing to stand for an hour or two.

TRAIN CLOSURE

The train system in Japan is primarily suited for the hours in which businessmen are active. For that reason, the last train typically runs at about 11:40pm, and then service stops again until 5:00am. If you intend to be out at a bar or club during non-active hours, you'll need to call a taxi. While Japan is generally considered a safe country, as in any place around the world, it's best to avoid walking in the dark.

JAPAN TRANSIT PLANNER

There are a number of apps online that will allow you to plan the quickest route to your destination, including number of stops, any transfers, train numbers, platform numbers, and other information you'll need to find your train quickly and easily. Check out Japan Transit Planner or any of a number of online resources provided by JR in order to map out your route on the go.

2.11 TRAVELING VIA BUS

In many cities—even large ones like Kyoto—the train system is not going to be able to get you to every location you want to visit. If this is the case, it's likely that a bus will be able to take you where you want to go.

EXPRESSIONS

DOKO DESU KA

Where is?

KORE KIYOMIZUDERA NI IKIMASU KA?

Does this go to Kiyomizu temple?

USJ NI IKITAI DESU

I want to go to USJ

USJ DE TOMARIMASU KA?

Does this stop at USJ?

WASUREMONO DESU!

I forgot something!

"WANT TO" DO SOMETHING

One of the expressions you've likely noticed repeatedly in the travel section is *ikitai*, or "want to go." This comes from the verb stem *iki*, which means "to go," and the ending *tai*, which means "to want to." The particle *ni*, which always comes before *ikitai*, indicates movement or direction, sort of like the preposition "to" in English.

KINKAKUJI NI IKITAI DESU

I want to go to Kinkakuji

[PLACE] NI IKITAI DESU

I want to go to [place]

ASKING ABOUT BUS STOPS

Just as *ikitai* is always paired with *ni*, *tomarimasu* is always paired with *de*.

KINKAKUJI DE TOMARIMASU KA?

Does this stop at Kinkakuji?

[PLACE] DE TOMARIMASU KA?

Does this stop at [place]?

SITUATION: FINDING THE BUS STOP

Sometimes you'll know that you need to get on a bus, but you won't be able to find the bus stop (in Japanese, *basu tei*). Thankfully, asking where to find it is a simple process.

SUMIMASEN

Excuse me

BASU TEI, DOKO DESU KA?

Where is the bus stop?

ASOKO DESU

It's over there

ARIGATOU GOZAIMASU!

Thanks so much!

EXERCISE: WHERE IS?

Take a minute to use repetition practice to memorize some of these travel-related phrases you might need.

[PLACE] DOKO DESU KA?

EKI	station
TAKUSHI NORIBA	taxi lane (the place where taxis wait for customers)
BYOUIN	hospital
KONBINI	convenience store

HOTERU hotel

SUUPAA supermarket

Note: be careful, because *byouin* means hospital, but *BIyouin* (with a long *bee* sound at the beginning) means beauty salon.

SITUATION: CHANGING BUSES

Sometimes, you might discover that you've boarded the wrong bus or need help figuring out where to go. Just like train station platforms are counted by *ban*, so are bus numbers.

SUMIMASEN

Excuse me

KORE, KIYOMIZUDERA NI IKIMASU KA?

Is this bus going to Kiyomizu temple?

CHIGAIMASU, IKIMASEN

No, that's not right, it's not going there

NANBAN DESU KA?

Which number is [going there]?

(13) JYUU SAN BAN DESU

Bus number 13

ARIGATOU GOZAIMASU!

Thanks so much!

If you are well and truly lost, one phrase that will come in handy is *michi ni mayotta*, or "I've lost my way." *Michi* is a road or path, and *mayotta* is the past tense of the verb "to get lost." If you want to ask someone for help, try *tetsudatte kuremasen ka?* This means "Would you be so kind as to help me?"

2.12 INTRODUCING AND TALKING ABOUT YOURSELF

While most Japanese people out and about on the street will not stop to ask you about your day or where you come from, there are plenty of situations in which you might find the need to introduce yourself and tell others a little bit about you. For example, maybe your taxi driver is being friendly on the way to your hotel, or maybe you're on a long train ride with a kind older Japanese woman who's interested in the book you're reading.

In Japan, foreigners are called *gaijin*, and while the attitude toward them varies depending on what context you're talking about, overall, people are very friendly.

EXPRESSIONS

MARY DESU	My name is Mary
HAJIMEMASHITE	Nice to meet you
[COUNTRY] KARA KIMASHITA	I'm from [country]
TONDEMO NAI DESU	No way

SITUATION: DISCUSSING LOCATIONS

Some country names are relatively similar in Japanese, and others different more significantly. Make sure you check up on your own country name before you go so that you'll be prepared to answer!

AMERIKA	America
OOSUTORARIA	Australia
NYUU JIIRANDO	New Zealand
KANADA	Canada
DOITSU	Germany

To say that someone is a person from a specific country, you can use the counter for people, *jin*.

AMERIKAJIN	American
KANADAJIN	Canadian
DOITSUJIN	German

SITUATION: SPEAKING IN JAPANESE

You may occasionally find that as you have these lighthearted conversations with strangers, they might be taken by surprise that you can speak Japanese!

KONNICHIWA

Hello!

HAJIMEMASHITE

It's nice to meet you

MARY DESU

I'm Mary

NIHONGO YOOSU DESU NE!

You're very good at Japanese!

NIHONGO, UMAI DESU NE!

Your Japanese sounds very good!

HOW TO RESPOND

If a Japanese person complements you on your Japanese language skills, one of the most culturally common ways to respond is by saying, "Oh, not at all!" or similar. It's generally considered good form to play yourself down when possible.

NIHONGO UMAI DESU NE!

Your Japanese sounds great!

TONDEMO NAI DESU!

Oh, not at all, no way!

EXPRESSIONS OF PRAISE IN JAPANESE

Sometimes, you may be greeted with people who give you compliments. A couple of Japanese words are very common in these situations:

KAWAII cute

KAKKOII cool

NIATTEIMASU to suit (as in "that shirt really suits you") or look good

SUGOI amazing

SITUATION: AN EXTENDED CONVERSATION

Here is what a more extended Japanese conversation might look like:

KONNICHIWA
Hello!

NIHONGO, DAIJOUBU DESU KA?
Is Japanese okay?

CHOTTO DAIJOUBU DESU
Sure, I can speak a little

OKUNI WA DOKO DESU KA?
Where are you from?

AMERIKAJIN DESU
I'm from America

RYOKOU DESU KA?
Are you a tourist?

HAI!
Yes!

NIHON WA DOU DESU KA?
How are you finding Japan?

TANOSHII DESU!
It's very fun!

As you may have noted, *ryokou* means to take a trip for the purposes of sightseeing or being a tourist.

SITUATION: YOU SPEAK JAPANESE WELL!

See if you can understand this common conversational narrative.

NIHONGO, DAIJOUBU DESU KA?

Is it okay to speak in Japanese?

CHOTTO, DAIJOUBU DESU

Sure, a little Japanese is okay

NIHONGO YOOSU DESU NE

Your Japanese is very good!

TONDEMO NAI DESU

Oh, no way

NIHONGO UMAI DESU NE

Your Japanese sounds very good

CHOTTO DESU

It's just a little

Umai is a word that, in the context of food, means "delicious" or "great." This meaning is similar to its use here as "very good." *Chotto* means "a little bit" and can be used both in terms of amount and, as in this conversation, to downplay something by essentially saying, "Eh, not really."

LIKES AND DISLIKES

As people get to know you, they may begin to question things you like and dislike—especially if you find yourself in a place where that might matter, like in a restaurant or when being served food at someone's house.

SUSHI, KIRAI DESU

I dislike sushi

SUSHI, SUKI DESU

I love sushi

Kirai means to dislike something, and *suki* means to like something. You may be asked whether or not you like *natto,* as many Japanese people often seem interested in whether foreigners enjoy this particular food. Natto is a type of fermented soybean that has a very strong smell. It's certainly worth trying!

Be aware when using *kirai* that it is a rather strong term that is more akin to "hate" than "dislike." Best not to use it when you've been served something at someone's house, for example. If you'd like to very gently say that you're not a big fan of something, try *suki ja nai* instead.

SITUATION: IN ENGLISH, PLEASE

Despite all your practice with Japanese, there will always end up being situations in which you're not entirely sure what's been said. In this instance, using *chotto wakarimasen* is an easy way to say, "I don't really understand." Again, it uses *chotto*, conveying that "little bit" idea to say "I don't really get it, but maybe I understand just a little bit."

SUMIMASEN

I'm sorry

CHOTTO WAKARIMASEN

I don't really understand

EIGO DE ONEGAI SHIMASU

Please say it in English

Wakarimasen means "I don't understand," and by itself, it's a great word to remember so that you can communicate when someone's lost you in their train of thought. *Onegai shimasu* is polite enough here to convey that you're sorry for any hassle you caused in having a hard time with comprehension.

2.13 EMERGENCIES AND ACCIDENTS

As much as you probably don't want to think about something bad happening during your trip to Japan, it's important to have a plan of action in case things go wrong. If you need to call the police or an ambulance, there are a couple important numbers for you to know.

EMERGENCY SERVICES IN JAPAN

- Police: 110
- Ambulance: 119
- Fire Department: 119

SITUATION: GETTING HURT

Imagine that you find yourself in a dire situation. Maybe you're walking down a dark alley late at night and meet a yakuza who pats you down for your wallet. Maybe you trip and fall while hiking up to a temple on the top of a mountain and can't walk. In these situations, you have a few options available to you.

- Listen and look around to see if any Japanese people are nearby who might help
- Call the police or an ambulance
- Continue on as if nothing happened

If you choose to interact with a person, either physically or via the phone, understand that most Japanese people are not taught a lot of English. Emergency personnel in particular are not ready to be your interpreters. So what do you do to get help?

OPTION 1: CALL EMERGENCY SERVICES DIRECTLY

If you choose to call 110 or 119 directly, you may wait for a short time before you're attended to so that the agency can locate where you're at.

KYUU KYUU SHA YONDE KUDASAI

Please call an ambulance

KEIKAN YONDE KUDASAI

Please call the police

The word for ambulance is essentially "QQsha" when pronounced, for ease of understanding. *Yonde kudasai* means "please call."

KAJI DESU

It's a fire!

If people begin to try to ask you questions about what is happening and you can't understand them, your best bet is likely *not* to try to explain (in Japanese) that you don't speak Japanese. Most native speakers will understand the phrase "No Japanese, sorry" and react accordingly.

OPTION 2: CALL A TRANSLATION SERVICE

If your complaint can wait a short time, you can call an interpretation service to assist you in making your emergency call.

03-5285-8185

Emergency medical interpretation service

03-3501-0110

Tokyo English Speaking Police

Specifically in Tokyo, there is a small branch of the police department that can handle calls in English because there are so many English-speaking tourists in the city. This service is available 24/7. However, remember that it is an emergency service; while police are very helpful people in general, this service is not to be used when you've gotten off at the wrong train station and need help finding your way back or even when you've lost your wallet (instead, head to the Lost and Found or the help desk inside the nearest station). Even a convenience store worker would be likely to help you in these situations.

SECTION 3: ADDITIONAL HELP

Congratulations, you've reached the end of your basic Japanese education for newcomers to Japan! If you don't feel 100% confident in your Japanese abilities yet, or if you're realizing that you've grown fond of Japanese and want to learn more, this section will give you more resources. Similarly, if there's an area you still feel weak in, the resources below will help to bridge your own personal gaps in an individualized manner that's best suited to you.

BEST BOOKS FOR LEARNING JAPANESE

When it comes to learning Japanese, one of the areas in which students often get the most frustrated is in reading and learning new words (or the kanji that go with them). It can be time-consuming to constantly need to switch back and forth between what you're reading and a dictionary to look up all the unfamiliar words. That's why textbooks and graded readers specifically geared toward helping new and long-time learners with their reading comprehension are so valuable! They both serve different purposes; while textbooks are intended to teach Japanese and form the foundation of your ability to read and write in the language, graded readers are tailored to individual skill levels to ensure that you improve in not only your speed but also your comprehension when reading Japanese.

However, there are a lot of products on the market about Japanese, including both textbooks and graded readers. Knowing that, it can be hard to see where to go next and which products are worth your time and money. In the realm of textbooks, there are a few common options that are considered the gold standard in Japanese education, and these would be a worthwhile place to start.

Genki

For those just starting out in Japanese, there's really no better place to start than Genki. Genki is the cornerstone of most Japanese learners' education, and for good reason. This series of textbooks can take anyone—even from a beginning level so new that they've never even heard Japanese before—and guide them all the way through mid-intermediate. This textbook has a little bit of everything that a Japanese language student would need to succeed: audio examples, reading practice, in-text samples, workbooks, and even online resources. The foundation that Genki provides to new learners will serve them well, and those seeking to boost their Japanese to a conversational level with thrive with Genki's instruction.

However, keep in mind that if you're aiming to go all the way to native fluency, Genki doesn't progress into the advanced level of Japanese language education. So, if that's what your goal is, you'll need to supplement your education with other options. It's a start, though, and students around the world would agree that it's one of the best. Because it's such a ubiquitous option for learning Japanese, consider checking your local library for a copy or see if they can get you a copy on loan so that you can check it out.

Tobira

As mentioned previously, while Genki is a powerhouse in Japanese education, it fails to progress students beyond the mid-intermediate level. Where are supposed to go after that? If you're seeking fluency in Japanese, you'll need to move on from Genki, and the most logical next step is to Tobira. Tobira tackles issues of advanced Japanese for those trying to inch closer to native fluency, and the much more immersive layout will enable learners to study Japanese *in* Japanese. Yes, students will be taking their education from native Japanese paragraphs. This naturally means that students are expected to have at least a passing understanding and mastery of kanji so that they'll be able to navigate the textbook. This helps to reinforce what's already been learned and improve fluency in an immersive way.

Unfortunately, and as is the case with many textbooks, one of Tobira's main downfalls is its lack of listening practice. After all, how is a textbook supposed to replace real live human interaction? There is no substitute for native immersion, so those opting for Tobira should expect to refer to podcasts, online shows, and other audiovisual media to bridge the gap in learning.

Speak and Read Japanese

For those who want to boost their Japanese by being able to read, write, and remember kanji—the complex characters Japanese is known for—one way to begin that adventure is by learning mnemonics. While many people feel that kanji are just a mess of lines, that's not actually true! Kanji have a logical and predictable pattern of creation and reading, and if you can begin to learn the secrets to how kanji are made, you'll very quickly be able to recall them and improve your Japanese comprehension. Mnemonics, or tricks with imagery and association, can be used to help your brain keep track of kanji and associate them with ideas that you are familiar with to assist memorization. This helps to keep the kanji in your head rather than allowing them to drop out of memory as time passes.

The entire purpose of Speak and Read Japanese is to create these kanji mnemonics to help learners make strong associations with Kanji. You may have found yourself wondering: how could someone ever remember the kanji for "bright?" What if you suddenly learned that "sun" and "moon" are the two pieces that make up this larger kanji? Now it's clear how this kanji might mean "bright" after all!

Nihongo Tadoku

Once you've gotten the basics of Japanese down from studies in textbooks and this guide, you'll be able to start tackling stories and even full-length books. Graded readers are the ideal location to begin at this stage. Graded readers are specifically crafted at levels ranging from absolute beginner to near native, and Japanese language learners will be exposed to new words in a carefully curated, repeated way to assist with context clues and word memorization over time. These stories meet Japanese language students where they're at, regardless of level, to help them improve their vocabulary and reading comprehension. One of the best places to begin in the world of graded readers is Nihongo Tadoku.

The books offered by Tadoku are available in a variety of types to suit the tastes of any student, from fairy tales to biographies and novels. This means that you'll probably be able to find a graded reader that's talking about a subject you're interested in, which is great; you'll be more likely to pay attention and learn from something that actually interests you. And because these readers contain kanji with furigana written above them to serve as pronunciation guides for new words, you'll be able to master the words you haven't learned yet as you read.

White Rabbit Readers

One of the main disadvantages of graded readers is that you often have to buy them in physical form—that is, as a book. Not to mention that since you're probably picking them up to help with your introduction to the Japanese language, the front covers might seem a little more childish than what you'd normally feel comfortable carrying around. If you're hoping to find graded readers you can carry around with you on your smart phone or tablet, White Rabbit is likely the best choice. These graded readers are also suited to any level from absolute beginner to advanced, and they offer a plethora of features that physical books can't, like narration from native Japanese speakers. Kanji have furigana to assist with pronunciation, and while stories have to be bought individually, they are very inexpensive, which makes them accessible. The app works with Android and Apple devices, so being on a certain platform won't keep you from enjoying graded readers.

If you're heading to Japan, it's at least a little bit likely that at least some facets of the culture interest you. If that's the case, mastering Japanese at a level greater than what you would achieve only through this guide can help you to enjoy Japan for everything it really offers. Maybe you have a particular manga you'd love to be able to read, but every time you take a look at it, you get overwhelmed by all the Japanese inside. Maybe you're interested in improving your Japanese language skills in general and are afraid that reading skills will be left behind as you go. Whatever your reason might be, both textbooks and graded readers are a worthwhile addition to your repertoire of Japanese educational materials. These tools will ensure that you build upon your Japanese skills organically, which will make you more proficient and confident over time.

ONLINE JAPANESE RESOURCES

As you prepare for your trip to Japan, you've likely come across a huge number of internet resources that tout that you can "learn Japanese in 30 days" or promise online video courses that guarantee you'll be fluent in just a couple of months. With all of these sorts of hard sell resources out there, it can be challenging to know for sure which resources are worth your time online. This presents a greater challenge than the in-print books discussed earlier, as you can hold those in your hand or look at their reviews on online stores. For online media—especially that you have to pay for, but even if not—understanding quality can be a lot tougher.

Thankfully, as the internet has blossomed over the years, so too has the outpouring of resources online for improving your Japanese language skills. As you consider which online tools you'll need in order to take care of the pain points in your own Japanese language ability, take a little while to consider a couple of important questions that will start you off on the right foot.

Was this book your first exposure to Japanese, and now you need to supplement what you've learned? Or did this book just cement and clarify which pieces of Japanese you need, but you even know a bit more than what was discussed here?

Are you willing to pay for resources, or do you need to stick to only the online Japanese language tools that are free? To what extent is cost a factor?

What are you struggling with as you consider your trip to Japan? Do you worry that you won't be able to pronounce things? That people won't understand you or that you won't understand them? That you'll struggle to read kanji?

How much time do you have before your trip? Can you make time for a daily study session, or do you need something flexible?

It's important to give some consideration to answering these questions before you decide which tools are going to be best for you. The internet contains dozens if not literal hundreds of resources you could tap into, and you won't have the time or attention span to check them all out. Here are just a couple that stand out above the rest as quality options, whether you're trying to just branch out into beginner Japanese or find the next step in your advanced Japanese language journey.

Lingodeer

If you've tried to take some online Japanese language courses online, you've probably heard of companies like Mango. Unlike most of these common language education companies, Lingodeer is unique in that it started out specifically with Asian languages. For this reason, it has an advantage in trying to teach you Japanese, as it is built with things like complex Asian characters and writing systems in mind. You'll find culture notes that will expand your knowledge of Japan alongside the Japanese lessons you're taking, and thanks to the immersion that Lingodeer offers, you'll come out with a more well-rounded understanding of context in Japanese. Native speakers are behind the audio production, ensuring that you have the best start possible for your listening practice. This option comes with an app as well, so you'll have more flexibility in learning Japanese according to your daily routine.

While Lingodeer is a great resource for beginners, that's essentially who it is geared toward: beginners. Those in the intermediate and higher categories will likely find Lingodeer lacking and will have to find a different tool to use. It's not right for everyone, but for those just getting started, it's worth checking out.

Pimsleur

For some people, the reason that they haven't had much luck so far in learning Japanese is because they have a hard time grasping material that they read online. For many, this is because they simply aren't visual learners. If you need audio instruction in order to really feel yourself improving in Japanese, Pimsleur is an option worth checking out. This language learning tool is notorious for its high-quality audio instruction, and the number of courses and lessons it offers is just massive. You'll find high-quality narration across various genders and skilled voice actors of all ages, and it comes equipped with a mode specifically for use in your car, so you can continue to learn Japanese during an otherwise rather unproductive part of the day: your commute.

Pimsleur is a solid option for bridging the audio gap that commonly occurs in self-study Japanese language learners.

Wanikani

Wanikani was a game-changer when it was first developed. Its unique approach to learning and retaining Japanese kanji revolutionized how Japanese language learners (and, surprisingly, even native Japanese people) studied and learned the Japanese characters needed in everyday life. This book previously mentioned the use of mnemonics, or visual associations, to assist in the memorization of kanji, and if that method works for you, Wanikani is probably the closest to magic you'll ever find. Packed full of (honestly pretty fun) games and an algorithm that learns from you, you'll find your online Japanese education adapted to your own personal learning style. The algorithm spaces kanji repetition at the rate that you need based on how frequently you get that kanji right or wrong; correct kanji become more and more spaced for review as it becomes clear that you're mastering them, while kanji you struggle with are pulled for questioning more often.

As you might expect, Wanikani's main strength is in the written aspects of Japanese. If you're struggling in areas, Wanikani might not help so much. But because the program builds upon the foundation of Japanese using kanji radicals and simple vocabulary, this resource is a very worthwhile place for beginners to start on the road to being able to read Japanese. If you struggle to make consistent time to study Japanese, though, Wanikani might not work as well for you. The algorithm spaces kanji very strategically, so skipping lessons by not logging in will only work to your own disadvantage.

Lang-8

Lang-8 isn't a Japanese resource as much as it's a great tool for continuing to improve your Japanese in a real, immersive setting. This realistic setting for genuine, natural conversation with native speakers is one of the most common aspects missing from learning Japanese, and it's one area where new learners—especially tourists—struggle when they go to Japan. When you sign up, you can immediately begin making friends with real people. If you choose, you can ask questions to others, but the most helpful tool is the diary function. You can write out a post in Japanese, and native Japanese speakers will come and offer suggestions for how to more accurately and correctly say what you've written. In exchange you can help them with their English (or another language you know!), since everyone is there to learn. It's a mutually beneficial relationship that puts you in contact with real people.

Unlike in real classes, you are never obligated to work with a certain person, and your writing can be on anything at all that you're interested in. This will encourage you to participate more, and the community overall is very wholesome and helpful. It can be easy to make new friends from around the world using Lang-8!

Denshi Jisho

All Japanese language learners are going to need a reliable dictionary at some point, and it can be tough to choose which one will work best for you. Some contain pictures, some are full of more words than average at the cost of an English translation, and so on. But nothing can really beat the reliable Denshi Jisho. This online dictionary is convenient, because you can access it from anywhere instead of carrying around a paperback version to reference when needed, and it's full of a huge variety of extremely helpful resources. You can type in both English and Japanese, which can be helpful if you've found a Japanese word whose meaning you want to know AND want to look up a Japanese word corresponding to an English meaning. Denshi Jisho allows you to type in any of the various writing systems; if you have hiragana and kanji on your phone, it will accept those, or you can simply type the romaji (English character) spelling of a Japanese word, and the dictionary will do its best to convert it and then search.

Because it's an online tool that works with touch-screen phones and other mobile devices, Denshi Jisho is also extremely helpful as a tool for drawing kanji. Many people come across the problem where they see a word and need to know what it means, but they have no idea how to pronounce the kanji in it, so they can't even begin to look it up. With Denshi Jisho, you can draw the kanji into the dictionary, and it will recommend as many kanji as it can that it thinks are close. From there, you should be able to build that word you're looking at and search for it! Denshi Jisho is free and highly recommended as a resource, even for people who have no interest in learning Japanese beyond what's necessary to get by. You'll be able to look up words in a flash when you need them.

Maggie Sensei

One of the toughest things about learning Japanese and improving your skills is that many educational resources are geared specifically toward students, and they may like "genuine" or "life-like" examples and individual pieces of grammar in favor of something more educational. That's not a problem with Maggie Sensei, an online resource based on a Japanese dog named Maggie (don't tell anyone, but it's actually her owner giving out the Japanese advice, not Maggie!) This easy to understand website has compiled a huge trove of grammar and structure points about Japanese and put them together in an accessible and friendly way, including tons of example sentences—and cute pictures of animals. This is an entirely free website, so you can check in with it whenever you're struggling to express yourself or figure out what someone meant when they were talking to you.

Plus, the site comes with a feature called Maggie's Room, which is essentially a large and bustling online message board where anyone—including you!—can ask Maggie questions about Japanese. She is always happy to provide clarification and help, and this means that you get personalized when you need it in a way that other resources just can't offer.

Rikaikun

If you're going to be doing a lot of browsing the internet while in Japan and want to use (or even need to use) Japanese websites, such as to book tickets, Rikaikun is going to be invaluable to you as a new Japanese learner. It's an extension that you can add on to your internet browser, and it will allow you to mouse over kanji and see not only what they mean but also how to read them. This works on basically any Japanese website on the internet, so you no longer have to fear navigating a Japanese website (or relying on Google Translate to get you where you need to go).

The extension will do its best to assist you with whole-sentence and phrase meaning as well, though its main and most helpful function is specifically with kanji. It's free, and it simply sits quietly in the background when you're not using it, so it doesn't get in the way. If you find that it IS popping up a bit more often than you'd like, you can always temporarily disable it and then turn it back on when you need it. It's free, so it's certainly worth a try so that you can see how much it will help you during your trip.

Slow News in Japanese

If your primary concern is that you're unable to focus and listen to Japanese with the level comprehension that you'd like, Slow News in Japanese might be able to help you with that. You get to learn more about what's going on in the world, which is an extra bonus, while you improve your listening comprehension skills in Japanese. This resource is exactly what it sounds like: you can have the news read to you in Japanese, but slowly, so that you have more opportunity to listen carefully and understand. While you can certainly do this listening across a number of devices, the browser-based version is perhaps a bit more helpful, because it contains a built in tool that, much like Rikaikun, lets you mouse over kanji to see how they're read and what they mean. This works with both words and phrases, so the website really tries to assist you in your Japanese comprehension. This resource is also free, like many of the others recommended here, so it's at least worth trying out.

While it may be true that online Japanese language courses are going to be valuable to many people, for you in particular who are looking at traveling to Japan as a tourist, the resources you need might be slightly different than those of a Japanese language student trying to, say, get a degree in the subject. If you've decided that you'd like to master

Japanese on a level greater than what this book is offering, these resources may be extremely helpful to you, but even if you'd just like to ensure you have a smooth and pleasant visit in Japan, there's no harm in trying out some of these helpful tools, because they're free and really might make your life a lot easier.

3.1 A GUIDE TO JAPANESE WRITING

If this trip to Japan is going to be one of your first exposures to the Japanese language as a whole, it's common to feel more than a little bit overwhelmed. Other people have probably told you by now that Japanese—and the other East Asian languages—are notoriously difficult for English speakers to master because *look at all those characters*.

The reason that people have this idea that Japanese is so hard is because it uses an entirely different alphabet than English. The Latin alphabet of English contains 26 characters, but Japanese uses pictographic characters called kanji (in addition to two other, smaller alphabets of shapes called kana). This puts Latin-based speakers at a disadvantage, because not only do they have to learn new words, grammar, and pronunciation but also entirely new alphabet. If you went to Spain but didn't know Spanish, at least you'd be able to read the words phonetically because Spanish uses the same alphabet. You could stumble through. Not so with Japanese.

Don't let that turn you off of going to Japan, though! The Japanese language is both methodical and logical in how it handles its written language; in fact, you'll never have to worry about which letters make which sounds like you do in English. Think of how the letter "g" in English can sometimes sound like "guppy" and sometimes like "gentle" and you have an idea of how inconsistent English is. Japanese doesn't fall prey to this issue; a letter will *always* make the same sound.

In Japanese, the "alphabet" is made of three separate but related branches: hiragana, katakana, and kanji. This is the entirety of Japanese; if you learn these, you know how to read all Japanese.

Hiragana

Hiragana is the backbone of Japanese. It's necessary in order to be able to create sentences at all, and as such, it's the most common place for new learners to start. Each of these characters stands in place of a sound, so they don't have any meaning aside from just being phonetic. Think of them as "letters" that spell out Japanese words. The only difference is that many of these "letters" are actually made up of small blends. You'll see what I mean.

A: あ (ah)

I: い (ee)

U: う (oo)

E: え (eh)

O: お (oh)

Japanese vowels don't go in the same A-E-I-O-U as English, which is sort of quirky. These are all the vowels; Japanese doesn't use Y as a vowel. These are all the single-letter pieces of Japanese aside from *n*, which is also by itself and is pronounced "n," not "en." Beyond these single-piece hiragana, all the hiragana pieces are actually a consonant and vowel put together. Even though that means that they're made of more than one *English* letter, they are just one *Japanese* letter (character). It makes more sense to look at these hiragana sounds in trees:

The A Tree

Wa	Ra	Ya	Ma	Ha	Na	Ta	Sa	Ka
わ	ら	や	ま	は	な	た	さ	か

The I Tree

Ri	Mi	Hi	Ni	Chi	Shi	Ki
り	み	ひ	に	ち	し	き

The U Tree

Ru	Yu	Mu	Fu	Nu	Tsu	Su	Ku
る	ゆ	む	ふ	ぬ	つ	す	く

The E Tree

Re	Me	He	Ne	Te	Se	Ke
れ	め	へ	ね	て	せ	け

The O Tree

Wo	Ro	Yo	Mo	Ho	No	To	So	Ko
を	ろ	よ	も	ほ	の	と	そ	こ

Then, there's that special *n* character.

N

ん

That's it! If you learn those hiragana, there will be literally nothing in Japanese that you can't spell out. Japanese is phonetic, not meaning-laden; in other words, unlike Chinese, where each character means something, Japanese hiragana is nothing but sounds that you use to spell out words.

At this point, you're probably both a little confused and a little worried. These aren't the big, complicated characters that you know Japanese is made of! You're right. The good news is that you don't actually *need* to learn those big characters at all! You probably want to at some point if you'd like for your Japanese to be more fluent, but if your primary concern is just being able to read and write, hiragana is your target. Big kanji like 頑張る (*ganbaru*, to try hard) contain much more complicated characters, but you don't need to worry; every single Japanese word can be "spelled out" in hiragana. If you write がんばる instead, people will understand what you said exactly as if you'd used kanji.

Katakana

Japanese took a lot of influence from early Chinese, which is why both languages contain characters (that actually often mean the same thing and sometimes are even pronounced nearly the same). One of the issues that Japanese people encountered when they started to work on really making Japanese their own was how to handle foreign words. There were a lot of words from other cultures that they found themselves using a lot, and they didn't want to make a brand new kanji for each one. So instead, they created a different alphabet—one that's neither hiragana nor kanji—that's intended specifically to write down these foreign loan words. This is called katakana, and it's used only for words that Japanese has borrowed from other languages.

At first, this may not seem like something worth knowing. After all, how often does Japanese really borrow words? As it turns out, actually fairly often. That's why most learners tackle katakana next, before kanji. Katakana is just like hiragana; it's made of the same 46 sounds. So, you essentially just have to learn two separate sets of 46 characters.

A: ア

I: イ

U: ウ

E: エ

O: オ

The A Tree

Wa	Ra	Ya	Ma	Ha	Na	Ta	Sa	Ka
ワ	ラ	ヤ	マ	ハ	ナ	タ	サ	か

The I Tree

Ri	Mi	Hi	Ni	Chi	Shi	Ki
リ	三	ヒ	二	チ	シ	キ

The U Tree

Ru	Yu	Mu	Fu	Nu	Tsu	Su	Ku
ル	ユ	ム	フ	ヌ	ツ	ス	ク

The E Tree

Re	Me	He	Ne	Te	Se	Ke
レ	メ	ヘ	ネ	テ	セ	ケ

The O Tree

Wo	Ro	Yo	Mo	Ho	No	To	So	Ko
ヲ	ロ	ヨ	モ	ホ	ノ	ト	ソ	コ

Then, there's that one "special" character: N.

N

ン

In this guide, you've already seen some katakana loan words like "coffee," which is *ko-hi-* in Japanese and so would be written as コーヒー. Remember, this alphabet is only for foreign words. You don't need to use it any other time.

Kanji

Yes, you knew it was coming; kanji, the large, complicated characters Japanese is most notorious for. The good news is that if you're going to be learning kanji, you actually don't need to learn each and every one individually. Instead, most kanji are made up of smaller pieces called radicals, and if you can learn the radicals, you can piece together not only how to write or read a kanji but also what it means. For example, let's take 親.

親 *oya* means "parents." But if you take a closer look, you might notice that this kanji is actually made up of a few parts, and each one can help us understand what the whole thing means. 立 *ta(tsu)*, on the top left, means “to stand.” Below *tatsu* is 木 *ki,* which is the word for “tree.” So far, it kind of seems like someone might be standing in a tree. The right side of the kanji starts with 目 *me*, which is “eye,” but the additional small legs underneath it make it 見 *mi(ru)*, “to watch.” So what sort of person might you find standing way up in a tree watching? Parents who are keeping an eye out for their kids! This is just one example of how understanding the individual pieces of a kanji might be able to help you piece together the whole. This way, you don't have to memorize every single kanji as if it's made up of pieces you've never seen before.

WHEN TO LEARN

While it's important to understand all three systems of Japanese writing, it can certainly be overwhelming to try to learn hiragana, katakana, and kanji all at the same time. For that reason, it's best to pace yourself and learn them in the order in which they'll be most helpful to you. Focus on making sure that people can understand you and that you can function within the society first, *then* turn your attention to refining what you know and what you're able to read and write.

Knowing that, it's generally considered best to start with hiragana as your first step. Because you need hiragana in order to be able to read anything in Japanese, it's a great place to begin, and it will also equip you with all the tools you need to be able to write out or say anything in the Japanese language. If you don't know what a kanji is or how to write it, you can spell it out in hiragana and be understood just the same. Japanese people know that not everyone who is reading will be able to read all kanji (think: Japanese schoolchildren who haven't learned those kanji yet), so many kanji you encounter will probably have small hiragana above them (called furigana) to assist with reading the kanji. They will show the pronunciation.

After you've had some time to get used to hiragana and are getting a grip on how it works, it makes sense to move on to katakana. If you just stop at hiragana, you'll find yourself unable to express certain thoughts if they require loan words; you might not think at first that this is such a big deal, but loan words are some of the most common pieces of vocabulary you'll be relying on in Japan. Words like taxi, coffee, and America are all written in katakana, so it's a good next step after you've spent some time with hiragana.

While you're learning both hiragana and katakana, it doesn't hurt to sprinkle in some kanji as you go. If you find a kanji that looks very simple (has just a couple strokes or seems easy to remember), maybe add it to a list. Easy kanji like "water" and "person" will end up being helpful and aren't too hard to remember. Once you feel that you have a better handle of hiragana and katakana, your focus can shift to learning radicals so that you understand how to piece together large kanji and take a guess at what they mean.

Japanese is by no means an easy language, but learning a new language in general is never going to be easy. With some effort on your part and a solid strategy of repetition and practice, you'll be able to both read and write in Japanese much more quickly than you might have imagined!

About Us

Welcome to JpInsiders, home of everything Japanese! If you're interested in the unique culture that this innovative and exciting country has to offer, we can offer you exactly what you're looking for and more.

Here at JpInsiders, we are experts in Japanese culture, and can satisfy your every need no matter what exciting area fascinates you.

Nestled in the heart of East Asia, Japan is home to one of the richest cultures the world has to offer, having pioneered an impressive range of concepts that have gained worldwide traction and popularity.

For example, Japan is the original home of anime and manga, the iconic Japanese cartoons and comic books that millions throughout the world have grown to know and love.

When it comes to the arts, Japan is forever developing new and exciting concepts. A whole host of popular crafts including bonsai, the art of growing miniature versions of trees or shrubs, and the intricate paper craft of origami both originated on Japanese soil.

Over the years, Japanese innovation has truly set a precedent that the rest of the world looks up to.

Whatever your personal interests, we are here to provide you with everything you may need to explore Japan's fascinating culture in greater detail.

We stock a range of books on everything from growing a bonsai tree to learning the Japanese language.

Or how about you get your hands on a great travel guide to help you pinpoint the must-see spots for your next visit?

Whether you are planning a memorable holiday in Japan, wishing to learn a brand-new skill, or simply intrigued by the country's wonderful culture, we will be delighted to help.

Explore our products and get ready to take in all the details you may like to know on Japanese culture.

If you have any question or query, please feel free to get in touch with us for more information. Immerse yourself in all the best and the most up-to-date details on this truly special country with the help of JpInsiders!

PS: Can I Ask You for a Quick Favor?

*First of all, thank you for purchasing **Learn Japanese Book for Beginners!** I know that you could have picked any number of books to read, but you picked this one and for that I am extremely grateful.*

If you enjoyed this book and found some benefit in reading it, I'd like to hear from you and hope that you could take some time to post a review if possible.

Your feedback and support will help me to greatly improve my writing craft for future projects and make this book even better!

THANKS!

=)

www.ingramcontent.com/pod-product-compliance
Lightning Source LLC
Chambersburg PA
CBHW070626310726
48982CB00001B/181
9781778131837